BORN WITH A
Broken Heart
AND THEN BLAMED FOR CRYING

An Autobiography by a Survivor

RHODA LANE

Copyright © 2021 by Rhoda Lane.

ISBN-978-1-6379-0182-3 (sc)

All rights reserved. No part of this book may be reproduced or transmitted in any form or by any means, electronic or mechanical, including photocopying, recording, or by any information storage and retrieval system, without permission in writing from the copyright owner.

The views expressed in this work are solely those of the author and do not necessarily reflect the views of the publisher, and the publisher hereby disclaims any responsibility for them.

Matchstick Literary
1-888-306-8885
orders@matchliterary.com

I have changed or omitted some names to avoid any more of the blame. How sad the people all of their lives who have no love to give. How blessed by God are the ones unloved when they learn to forgive.

CHAPTER 1

From a very long time ago, I thought I would like to be a writer. My brother wanted to be a reporter. But my writing, at least this book is going to be about myself, not other people.

Through the years when I would say something about my life several different people would say you should write a book. Well I'm going to do that now at 75 years old. Don't think it will be boring because of my age. My life has been anything but boring. In fact it's surprising I'm still alive.

We grew up in a small town in the Midwest I will call Gravelton. Our parents grew up here too. It's strange how many people stay in a small town like this or come back like I did. I had a chance to get away and stay away. But a beat down person always makes bad decisions because they think they're not as good as other people. I was first introduced to the blame game by my mother if you can call her that.

You see, she blamed me for being born. From the Time I was a very small child she would yell at me saying "your dad knew I was going to leave him when I got Danny Mark in school. That's why he got me pregnant with you," emphasizing the you as her voice got louder. My brother Danny was five years older than me and back then kids started first grade at five. I can't even dare to guess how many times mom screamed that at me. It was always the same words exactly over and over. I heard it so many times it was embedded in my brain.

So I thought the constant arguing and fighting was my fault. I even thought I was so bad that the devil would come and get me at night. I forced myself to stay awake all night. I thought the devil couldn't possibly get me in the daytime. I would lay real still with my head covered up till daylight. When I felt like I couldn't breathe, I would make a little tunnel so I could get some air.

Years later, I was diagnosed with chronic insomnia and I think forcing myself to stay awake all night every night must've caused it. In all my school pictures I had dark circles and bags under my eyes. When you don't go to sleep until daylight and have to get up at seven to get ready for school you are sure to have dark circles.

I grew up thinking if your own mother can't love you, no one ever will. You are unlovable. I'm still sure the arguing didn't just start after I was born. I'm sure she was mad from the time she found out she was pregnant. It has now been proven that babies can hear when they are in the womb. So it's no wonder I was born crying and cried for six months without stopping. My aunt said when she came in the door, mom would hand me to her and walk away. I must've been born with a broken heart.

CHAPTER 2

When I was a baby everyone who knew our family talked about how long and how bad I had colic. No one ever knew a baby having it for six full months. Of course she nursed me. Everyone did back then. I think even as a baby I must have sensed the hatred but you know in a way now I feel sorry for her. I chose to nurse my babies when most people didn't. I loved it even though people questioned me about it. I knew it was the best for them and it was our special time together. I try to imagine my mom looking down at me while nursing me and knowing that nursing me was the only thing keeping me alive when she hated me.

Even though I will never be able to understand how you could hate your own baby, I still feel very sorry for her. Her feelings for me never changed even though I was a perfect child and a pretty little girl. Some older women told mom that my hair looked like spun gold. I have daddy's green eyes though and I'm sure she hated that too. I had an aunt who would never allow kids in her living room but she told mom I could come in there. Now you might think that a mother would be proud when an aunt said that and bragged on me saying what a good little girl I was. Not my mom. She said "well she better be she knows better." I think right then my aunt saw through mom because she went in the bedroom and came out with a beautiful opal necklace that matched her earrings. She said she didn't wear it much and since our birthdays were in the same month I could have it. I just kept looking at it and her. I couldn't believe she actually gave it to me and she kept smiling. And I still have it.

CHAPTER 3

Not long ago, I asked my primary doctor to send me somewhere for testing because I was forgetting things and I thought I was getting Alzheimer's. So she sent me to the psychologist who gave me a test that lasted four hours. I had taken a similar test 10 years before. But let me back up and explain a little. I had started having tremors in my face. A local neurologist tested me and said they were just undetermined tremors. Later I heard about another neurologist that had a better reputation so I went to her. When I told her what the first doctor said she acted upset and said well it has a name. It is Miege syndrome. Then she ordered an MRI. The diagnosis was cerebral vascular disease of the brain. Hardening of the arteries. Then she sent me for a test that lasted most of the day.

I scored 99% on the test of people in my age group who didn't have the disease. Then the second test I was so concerned there was something wrong that I didn't really try very hard. The doctor said to bring someone with me for the results. I took my daughter. This doctor scored the test like they did in school. He showed us a large graph he said on one end it looks like I could have problems but on the other hand I couldn't have a problem because of my IQ (intelligence quotient) was 130. I was surprised. I knew my IQ in high school was over 100 but not that high. I guess you get smarter as you age.

The doctor said on the test the lower end was depression like that was a simple thing. I have taken medication for depression most of my adult life. When you are raised by a mother who makes you think you're nothing, you develop a habit of being depressed. I had always known that my dad and brother were really smart but I was so beat down by my mom. I think I just used all my skills to survive. I was afraid of my mom and I knew not to tell anyone how bad she treated me. My second husband told me that I am my own worst enemy. He said you blame yourself for everything. When you've been told that all your life you believe it. The blame game it's called the scapegoat in the Bible.

CHAPTER 4

It's hard for me to call my mom, Mom. She didn't want me and she made that really plain. No matter how hard I tried, I couldn't get close to her. She put me down about everything I did. I could always feel the hatred and see it in her eyes. She was very controlling and domineering and those are the nice words for her. In fact, she was mean and evil. And she lied. Some of the things she told us about her childhood might not be true.

I was very intuitive, even as a child, so when her brother, his wife and mom would sit across the room staring at me and he would say "if you wanna dance you have to pay the fiddler" in a joking way. I knew what he meant. They thought I was too young and dumb to figure it out but I knew.

Years later the same aunt told me that after I was born mom told them that her life was over and she was in mourning for her own life. She said for the next few years mom only wore black, navy blue, and dark purple. Mom was 24 when I was born and 29 when I started school at five.

She could have left Daddy then and she lived to be almost 88. So her life was not quite over at 24, right? Planning to leave daddy was just another lie, so she would have something else to use against us. Torture that's what it was. I tried so hard to please mom but never did anything right as far as she was concerned.

CHAPTER 5

My dad and brother were both good to me but she was the boss and the controller. So if daddy paid attention to me, it made her mad and she would treat me or him worse. Daddy would try to protect me when she would be yelling at me. He would say "leave her alone. She's had enough," That made her turn on him. Then he would walk into the kitchen with her right behind him telling him that she would say anything she wanted to say to me and it was none of his business. Then he would glance at me out of the corner of his eye and I realized he had saved me again. They would argue for hours.

She had her own names for him too. It was always you dirty little no good slant shouldered son of a bitch. One of his shoulders was a little lower than the other. Scoliosis. I have it too. Also one daughter and one grandson of mine has it. Some people tell me to forget the bad things in the past and move on but with mom almost everything was bad. She hated everything. I know I have to forgive because God says I have to. It's not easy and forgetting is impossible. Believe me I've tried. I think writing it down might help. My older sister is starting to forget things now at 83. Hopefully she will forget how bad mom treated us.

CHAPTER 6

I'll go back now to what I have deduced from things I've been told. My parents grew up during the Depression. Daddy was six years older than mom. Her dad was dying and he liked daddy. He told mom he wanted her to have someone to take care of her before he died. So I'm sure he encouraged what happened. Our parents were married in 1933 and had my sister in 1934 almost exactly 8 months to the day.

My older sister told me one day that she was going to ask mom why she treated her so bad but when I told her what I have said here she agreed and didn't ask mom. Mom got even with her though. Why else would she name her such a horrible name? Zelphia. She hated her name as a child but later realized it didn't matter. I don't know who named me but it's not bad, Rhoda Lane.

CHAPTER 7

Our parents had another baby when I was seven and Zelphia was 14. Mom let Zelphia name her and then expected her to pretty much raise the baby while her and daddy ran around with another couple who were friends. They would go to this fancy bar where they were entertained by two piano players. I guess mom could drink in the open there. You see she and her brother were closet drinkers. I always knew where they hid it though. I guess I was either too observant or too nosy. Really it's pretty hard to hide gallon size jugs. They both had red noses too. You would have to drink a lot of wine to turn your nose red.

Meanwhile at home, Zelphia's boyfriend would come to the house when she was there taking care of the baby. Finally the inevitable happened. They started having sex. When mom found out she treated Zelphia like trash. She screamed at her for hours. The most prevalent memory I have of Zelphia is her standing beside the coal stove with mom beside her screaming at her with my sister's head hanging down and her tears hitting the linoleum floor. The abuse just went on and on. Daddy, Zelphia and I were mom's targets. Any parent should have known better than to leave a 14 or 15-year-old with her boyfriend at the house. My sister was a child and our parents were to blame not her. The coal stove was in the middle room of the house. Now I'll tell you about the rest of the house.

CHAPTER 8

The kitchen was large so the table was in there. The middle room was supposed to be the dining room but mom had to act important so she had made the middle room the everyday living room. The living room was the fancy living room that was hardly used. One of the two bedrooms was for our parents. The other was Zelphia's and mine. The baby slept with our parents then eventually daddy was pushed to the couch. My little sis slept with mom till she got married.

The fancy living room had a rollaway bed in one corner for my brother but it had to be folded up every day with a pretty flower cover on it just in case someone important knocked on the door. No one used the front door. Everyone came in the back door through a little porch into the kitchen.

My brother didn't say anything about his sleeping arrangement until years later. Then one day when we were talking about our childhood he said "I never had a bedroom." I could tell it really bothered him so that formal living room was just a waste when it could have made my brother happy. Maybe that was partly why he was hardly ever at home. He had lots of friends and just ran around town most of the time. We didn't have snacks at home. Sometimes we would eat a raw potato sandwich with butter and mustard. Or perhaps a cold bean sandwich with mustard. Sometimes Danny would beat up raw eggs and bread and then sometimes Danny would get his frog gig that he had made with an old stick and old fork. Then he would go to the frog pond just outside of town. Before long he would come home with several frogs. He would clean them out by the alley, bring in the legs in the kitchen and fry them. Oh! And they do jump in the skillet. If Danny didn't have friends with him he would share them with me. Yuck! But I ate them because Danny did. Danny was the lucky one though because if mom started yelling at daddy, Zelphia or me, he would just leave. Mom didn't try to stop him. I guess because he was a boy.

CHAPTER 9

Even after we were all married mom never stop trying to turn us against daddy. She would just come to our house unannounced and uninvited and stay as long as she wanted. Zelphia told me one time at her house mom just kept on and on until she just couldn't take it anymore. She said she slammed her fist on her kitchen table and told mom shut up or get out and don't come back. That shut her up for good at Zelphia's house but not mine. After my ex insisted we moved back to Gravelton it really got bad. I didn't want to move back. I knew it would be bad. Because my parents had moved back.

CHAPTER 10

One time I was fixing Rachel's hair for school and I was so nervous with mom watching. She came every morning just to spite me. I told Rachel I was very sorry I couldn't get the part straight. Mom said no wonder you're not holding the comb right. Did she really think that everyone in the world but me held a comb like her? That's the kind of crazy stuff we had to listen to from her. None of us were close to her except little sis. Mom knew it was her last chance so she treated her better. But she ruined her life too. After daddy died, she just gradually moved in with Sis and her husband until Sis finally became a clone of mom.

When we were kids, sometimes I would say mom you know she's lying and mom would say leave her alone so now she is just a habitual liar. I thought of a couple of other things I might as well put in here. I was allowed to just run around town when I was too young to get pregnant but not too young to get molested and I did. Anyway someone gave me a punch card where you sell punch offs and one person wins something. It happened to be a doll with a little golden braids and then I got one so I started selling the punch outs. Mom got mad but she let me finish but when I got the doll it just disappeared. Then another thing my cousin made me a Snow White and seven dwarfs cut out things in shop class. It was real pretty. He painted it nice colors. It disappeared to. Strange. Right? She claimed to know nothing about it either.

CHAPTER 11

My brother hurt his leg once bailing hay but didn't tell anyone until it was so infected he could barely walk. He knew he needed a doctor but we all knew mom didn't like to spend any of the big wad of money she kept pinned in her bra. When I fell and broke my nose, she just told me to put a wet washrag on it. When the neighbor boy stuck a weed cycle in my leg because he didn't want me climbing the tree that separated our yards. Even though the blood was running from just below my knee to my foot she wouldn't even look at it. Just get a washrag. She was more interested in screaming at the neighbor for leaving their tools out.

CHAPTER 12

When I started getting infected teeth at 11 mom called them gum boils and I didn't know any better. She just said get a needle and open them. But there was so much poison in them they would just swell back up. I kept opening them until I was past 13. One night my aunt and uncle came in when I was opening one of them. My aunt asked me to let her see and then she said she would make me a dentist appointment the next day. I had to take antibiotics then three molars had to be pulled. They were rotten all the way to the gums. One was filled. Do you think mom offered to pay? Of course not. She was going to let me die. There was a woman in our town who did die from infected teeth. Her two little kids were in the room when it happened.

CHAPTER 13

When I was 15 I got appendicitis. Probably from all the leftover infection from my teeth. My stomach has been hurting a lot but one Saturday night it got really bad. I didn't say anything until Sunday morning. Mom said it was just something I ate. But when it got worse later in the day she did get me an ice pack. We didn't have a family doctor so daddy kept going next-door to call different doctors. Then late in the evening it got so bad I told daddy he had to get me someone even if it was Oscar. He was an old man who walked to town every day from the country. That time daddy did talk the Dr. into seeing me. By that time my aunt and uncle had stopped by. But my little sister had the measles and I knew mom wouldn't want to leave. I had been blamed for her getting them because I had them first. Sis was in school and the school was full of them but it was still my fault (Blame Game).

Anyway mom and drunk crazy uncle took me to the Doctor Who said it was ready to rupture. So they took me to the hospital. As soon as they got me in a room the surgeon walked in. The doctor must have told him it was a real emergency because he had about three times as far to travel as we did. The surgeon said it would be just a few minutes so I told my mom to go on home. I know she wanted to because little sis had the measles. By this time in my life I had learned to be tough. I wouldn't let them put me in a wheelchair and the pain was getting worse but I wasn't even afraid. They gave me ether so I spent the next two days vomiting. The third day, three boys from school skipped and hitchhiked to come see me.

CHAPTER 14

Now going back to before Zelphia was raising the baby and even before I went to the movies by myself. When I was three or four Zelphia and Danny would go to the movies with me. Mom always sat in the car. Someone said she had a man who stopped and talked to her. Daddy would go in the back room of a bar just down the street to play cards. When the movie was over we would walk to the car and my siblings were willing to sit in the car and wait for daddy. But patience has never been one of my virtues so I would have them lift me up to a little window in that little back room that was always open even in the winter (probably to let the smoke out/the men all smoked). Most of the men would watch for me and say, "there's your little girl." Daddy would look up with his pretty green eyes that matched mine and say, "I'll be right out."

Born with a broken heart and then blamed for crying

CHAPTER 15

The ride home was always scary. I think that's why my siblings stopped going. Daddy always drove there so he had the car keys. But mom would try to get him to let her drive. When he wouldn't, she would keep grabbing the steering wheel and try to make him stop. I would hide between my siblings in the floorboard of the car. I always thought them arguing was my fault. The car would careen back-and-forth with her yelling at him the rest of the way home. I always thought maybe if I hadn't been born they wouldn't be arguing. Then when we got home she would push him and they would keep arguing. Most of the time we went to bed hearing and woke up hearing it.

CHAPTER 16

When my siblings quit going I went in the movies by myself. I learned all about the old times Cowboys and loved them. I didn't think about it at the time but being alone in the dark theater was not at all safe for a small child. My siblings teased me about my favorite Cowboy saying he was so skinny he had to wear two pair of underwear to find any clothes to fit him.

CHAPTER 17

When I went to the movies by myself was Friday nights. But then on Saturday night I would stay with grandma (Daddy's mom). I loved being with her. She was so much different than mom. She would put her arm around me and let me snuggle up to her while we looked at her picture albums or sang church hymns. Then she would put the tops from coffee sacks in my hair to curl it.

She would take them out in the morning before we went to Sunday school and church. She was the one who made sure I knew all about Jesus. I wouldn't have made it through my life without knowing Jesus. After church we would go back to her house and she would start cooking. I would ask her who was coming and she always said she didn't know but someone always comes. And they always did.

Just throughout the day different family members drifted in and out. Most of the time we would go out in the yard and she would kill three chickens. I would try to help her pluck the feathers from them after they were dipped in buckets of boiling water from the end of her cookstove that kept the water hot. But I was so little even when I held one up as high as I could reach, the neck was touching the ground. Grandma would pluck two then help me finish mine. I always wanted her to kill that big red rooster that was so mean and almost as big as me.

Every time I went to the outside toilet he would come after me. I would holler at grandma and she would chase him up into the woods with the broom. Grandma was a loving woman. She loved all her grandkids but seemed to take a special interest in me probably because she could tell how mom felt about me. It was pretty obvious I think to her and my aunts could see through mom. Everybody loved grandma. Danny always said she was the best woman he ever knew. I think Danny thought I was like her until

I did something that disappointed him. I told him how sorry I was but he shouldn't put me on a pedestal that I was just human. I had a couple of what people called funny uncles too but it wasn't funny. One of them always wanted me to sit on his lap even when I was way too old. I always tried to avoid him but I was never alone with him. The other uncle was worse but I'll talk about him in another chapter.

CHAPTER 18

I NEED TO TALK ABOUT SOME of my aunts. I had several who I realize now must've known how mean mom was because they would bring me things. Also they would talk mom into letting me go home with them for the weekend or longer in the summer. Daddy's oldest sister came the summer I was 11 and asked if I would like to make some money. Mom let me go home with her for two or three weeks. My aunt taught me how to paste for her to hang wallpaper. She pasted the first two strips and then I did the rest. She was amazing. She would put a board between two ladders and walk across to do the ceilings. She never looked down. We worked at three houses doing more than one room in each. She said I was as good at pasting as any adult she had ever worked with. I wasn't used to anyone bragging on me and she paid me. I had my own money. I developed a love for wallpaper.

Mom hung too but she had a woman paste for her. She would have never trusted me or gave me money. I started wallpapering in the houses we lived in when I got married. Later when I was homeless, I did that for other people. I painted inside houses also and outside and cleaned for people. I didn't have to advertise, I had a waiting list just by word-of-mouth.

Here's another story. I started cleaning and wallpapering for an older man. I had worked for him for a long time when a mutual friend told me he was in love with me. I had suspected it by some of the things he said but anyway she said he had me in his will. We took him to the doctor a few times when he didn't want to go by himself. Then another woman, I'll call her Jezebel, figured it out he had money and started after him. She told me I didn't need to take him to the doctor she would do it. I worked for her too and she wasn't like he thought. She acted sweet in front of him but when I worked for her she was always cussing and yelling at her dogs.

Anyway she fooled him and five months before they were both killed in a car wreck. She made him change his will leaving everything to her. What I don't understand is the man who drove them to the doctor said she died instantly and the older man reached out to him talking and smiling. How could everything go to her if she died first? Goes to show you what kind of person you shouldn't be!

CHAPTER 19

Back to my aunts, one aunt and uncle lived around 100 miles from us and they would come quite often and spend weekends with us. This aunt would bring a brown grocery bag of my older cousin's clothes for me almost every time. They were always real nice and about all I had. There was no fighting when they were there mom acted like a human being.

Since we only had two bedrooms, my aunt, cousin, sister and I also laid in the same bed but we slept side to side instead of up-and-down. My uncle and their little boy slept on the couch. This aunt was always laughing and taking pictures. I loved it when they were around. I always thought this must be what it's like to be a normal family.

One time she brought me a chocolate egg in a real pretty flower box. After I ate it, I put the box in one of the two drawers where all my clothes were except for a few in the closet. When my mom saw it one day she told me to throw it away. I tried to hide it but she found it and made me throw it away otherwise I might still have it. It was purple with all kinds of flowers on it.

Another sister of daddy's moved back home when I was in sixth grade. She had two restaurants in the city where she had lived but now bought a grocery store and the house next to it. She didn't like to stay alone so I got to stay with her. The house had a fireplace in the living room that I loved but it was really heated by the coal furnace that heated the store too. It had to be fired one more time before we went to bed. I would always go with her through a big garage then down to the basement where the big old furnace was located.

It was very scary but I don't think my aunt was afraid of anything. You can bet I was never more than two feet from her. I had to move over a little for her to use the big long shovel to fire the furnace. She was really strong too, just like daddy, her brother. I was surprised when mom let me stay with her then but now I know why. Daddy was out of work so he helped her run the store. I know now she paid him in groceries. Each day after school I went to the store and my aunt would tell me to pick out what I wanted for supper. Then she would tell me how to cook it and I would have our supper ready when she closed the store. She ran the meat counter and daddy ran the cash register. She was very particular about the meat and even ground her own hamburger. I also remember if she didn't go get her own meat and the slaughterhouse employees brought it, she would make them wait until she inspected it before telling daddy to pay them.

She was on a bowling team and bowled in that town where the movie theater was so I still got to go to the movies on her bowling night and at least one night a week to practice. She was good to me and since the bowling alley was just across the street from the theater, I would walk over there when the movie was over. She gave me money for the movie and even popcorn. Then in the bowling alley, she would give me money for a milkshake. She taught me to cook several things even casseroles. Mom never bothered to show me anything.

I almost forgot this… There was another bar where daddy played cards sometimes when I was younger. Ten cent rummy. This bar had a family room so when mom would take me in there to get daddy we would sit down in one of the big booths. Daddy always saw us come in and he would come up to that room and always sit with me on my side of the booth. Mom would order a Coke, daddy a champagne velvet beer, and I would say, "daddy can I have a milkshake?" He would always say yes and I don't know if it was just because daddy bought it for me or not but it seemed like that woman could make the best milkshakes in the world. I know it wasn't because I was a connoisseur of milkshakes but I would be so happy sitting with daddy drinking my milkshake until I raised my head up and looked at mom glaring at us. That's when I would start thinking about the ride home. That's probably the nights, I threw up. Danny threw up a lot too. He would just go outside but I hated it so bad I would try to hold it back too long and end up having to ask mom for a bucket. She would get it for me though. I don't know why I always asked for a milkshake. Anything daddy did for me made her furious and the ride home was even worse than usual. Then she would tell me her other famous lie. "Your dad don't want any of you kids. He just wants me."

CHAPTER 20

I GUESS I REALLY GOT OFF track, I was telling you about my aunts. The aunt that brought me the clothes from my cousin was married to one of my mom's brothers. The aunt that saved my life by getting my teeth fixed was married to my mom's other brother. She was also the one who told me mom said her life was over and went into mourning for her own life because I was born.

There is a lot more about them in another chapter but I'll tell this part now. This aunt and I were real close and my uncle told me I was the closest thing to a daughter she would ever have. Then my youngest sister told her that I was always mean to her when we were little. When my aunt told me she said that I told my aunt that was a lie. I said, "you know mom would have killed me if I was mean to her." She knew more than anyone else, but daddy how much mom hated me. I don't know why but it seems like people believe liars instead of truthful people. It really hurt my feelings and I thought my aunt was smart enough not to believe her lies.

Daddy's oldest sister was the one who taught me to wallpaper. The second sister was the one who owned the grocery store. The youngest was the one I didn't know as well because they traveled a lot for his work. Her husband wasn't very likable and always acted like he was better than us small-town people. He made a lot of money traveling but that didn't make him any better.

There is a funny story about him though that we all loved. A man had given Danny a beautiful black dog. From the day Danny got him, they were best friends. The dog followed him everywhere and chased every dog in town if they got close to Danny. Anyway when that aunt and uncle came to visit one time the uncle had a full-grown Great Dane dog and it was huge. Danny's dog was just medium size and the first thing my uncle said to Danny was, "you better watch your dog." A couple of days later as Danny was walking past grandma's house that big dog came out to the road. We all wondered if the uncle let him out on purpose but in a few minutes Danny's dog had the huge dog down on his back and was over him growling. Danny had to call him off. That smart alec uncle never said another word about dogs.

Now to my last aunt. She was mom's sister, but they were as different as night, and day. Mom thought cards were evil, and would never let us have them. But when I got to go to her sister's house, she taught me to play Solitaire. She would sit in her rocking chair facing the road, while I played cards at her desk. Then when she saw mom come down the road, she would say, "put the cards away. Here comes your mom." I would open the top drawer and push the cards in it then run over and sit on the couch.

She was my favorite aunt. They had a calf that they had gotten when it was real little. They were raising it for food. I don't know if I didn't understand, or just didn't want to, but I made a pet out of him. I had a straw cowboy hat so when the calf got big enough, I would wear my hat and ride him like a horse. As soon as he saw me, he would run over and nuzzle me. As he got bigger, my aunt had to lift me up on him. Then the fateful day came to butcher him. My dad helped, for some of the meat, but I wouldn't eat a bite of it. For several days, I wouldn't go to their house. All I did was cry. Some people tried to explain it to me but I just cried. To me he was a pet and I really missed him. I have a picture of him nuzzling my leg when I was eight years old.

CHAPTER 21

Mom had another thing she told me over and over. She said every time daddy was taking out the ashes from the coal stove, I would squat down beside him and say, "what you doing Daddy?" She said he would always say, "get the hell out of my way." But she said I kept doing it. But I don't think I would have been dumb enough to keep doing it, if he really said that.

CHAPTER 22

THE AUNT THAT OWNED THE grocery store, told me a neat story about when they were kids. Daddy, her and another sister were the three youngest of grandmas seven children, except the baby. My aunt said, we three little ones, stood up on one side of the table. We would always give your dad, the yolks from our eggs, because we knew, he liked them best. I think Daddy was everyone's favorite, because he had something the old folks called brain fever.

Grandma must have kept him out of school all that year because he didn't graduate until 1929. This isn't the most important thing he did though. He was baptized in the creek in January, when he was 23. They must have had to break the ice. The next year, his sister was baptized there too, also in January. He and Mom were married but she never went to church. That must have been when they held revivals.

CHAPTER 23

THERE WAS A CHILDLESS COUPLE in our town and every time he would see me with Mom he would ask her to let him and his wife have me. I think he could tell how scared and miserable I was, and he thought it would encourage me to know that someone wanted me.

I never said anything, but would always think maybe next time she will say yes. That is so sad for a child to think that way. I also wished she would leave me with Grandma. She had left Zelphia with Grandma when she was in first grade. Daddy was working out of town so, of course, mom had to be there to control the money. Mom told crazy stories. She said she even ironed Zelphia's socks. I wondered if she told Grandma to iron Zelphia's socks.

Mom must have taken Danny with her but he probably wanted to stay with Grandma. He really loved Grandma. Everyone loved her except mom. She talked bad about Grandma but I don't think Mom liked anyone. Grandma was good to everyone. Mom shouldn't have talked about her behind her back. Danny also loved our great grandpa. He was a good looking old man with snow white hair and a mustache. My brother's hair was white like that the last few years of his life. He has been gone two years now.

CHAPTER 24

My dad died young, only 63, after his eighth heart attack. His first one was at 43. I was 13 and since he had to recuperate at home, I would hurry home from school to ask him to squeeze my hand as he grew stronger. That's when I found out his hair wasn't black. He had always worn it long and combed back with hair oil, but it had to be cut short since he was in bed a lot. I was surprised to find out it was blond and curly. I would brush it, it was so pretty, I knew Mom didn't like it but she was always mad about something anyway. She didn't need a reason, she tried all her life to turn us against Daddy. It didn't work with we three older kids. Even after he died she would keep telling my little sis she was his favorite. She just could not shut up.

CHAPTER 25

Everyone knows that someone with a bad heart needs rest, and Mom knew it too, but she just would not let him. When he would lay down across the bed she would say get up, and when he didn't she would say, "I said get up." Then when he didn't, she would say, "get up or I'll turn the damn bed over." So he would get up, and go lay down in the yard, on an old blanket, with one of our old pillows Grandma made from a feather bed. That's where we got all our pillows.

CHAPTER 26

Daddy's first heart attack was in the woods, rabbit hunting with one of my cousins. He almost had to carry daddy out of the woods. My uncle, my cousin's dad, lived way out of town, down a washed-out lane. If my cousin hadn't been there, daddy wouldn't have made it by himself. I know this shouldn't go here but when we were at my uncle's all of us cousins wood swing on a great big Grapevine over a deep ravine. If it had broken, one of us wouldn't be here.

Now back to the heart attacks. One of his worst ones was in Hammond. He had a clot 3 inches from his heart. And even though he asked everyone when I was coming I couldn't go in, because if the clot had moved, before they got it dissolved it would have killed him. So I sat in the waiting room for three days. Then when I finally got to see him they would only allow one person in at a time. When I walked in he said, "Oh! you look so pretty" I was wearing a turquoise suit and he like the color. And since Mom wasn't in there, we had a real nice visit. Even though I was the only one he asked for, Mom still said my little sis was his favorite. Hello!!!

She was so mean, she spent her whole life trying to turn us against each other. I knew daddy loved me, but if he showed it in any way, it sent her into another tirade.

When my ex and I ran a service station, the owners tried to hire me to go to their other 125 stations in four states to teach the managers, how to do the book work. They said they would pay me well, and pay all my expenses, since I was the only one who knew how to do it right. This was when computers were a new thing. One time they said I was $0.04 off, then called the next day, and said I was right. The computer was wrong. But I had to turn their offer down because my babies were only two and four. I knew I couldn't be away from them for too long. And besides my first husband was insanely jealous. I knew I'd have to answer for it.

CHAPTER 27

I WAS SO NAÏVE BACK THEN that I never thought about having my name put on the agreement. Therefore I would have more on my Social Security check. But it was just in his name while I did the most work. He pumped gas daily until four when he had a teenager relieve him. He would go back to close the station after he ate supper and took a nap. I took care of the babies, kept an immaculate house, always cooked and did the bookwork banking and shopping for the station.

I stayed up late to do the book work and count the money. To make sure everything balanced. The amount of gallons had to coincide with the amount of gas showing on the pumps. Also with the amount of gallons shown on the stick when the gas left in the tank in the ground was measured.

A lot of times I had to do the book work over the next morning because he hadn't read either the pumps or stick right. I would have gone to the station and done it myself if I hadn't had two babies. When I had to do it over after he called with the new numbers, I had to hurry because I had to get the owner's money deposited in the bank before they started to wonder.

Most of the time he took the weekends off but my part had to be done every night. I guess it was all worth it though. I love my babies more than my own life. Back then I always cooked a big meal on Sunday like my grandma and I always baked pies too. Every Sunday, like clockwork, my ex's brother, wife, and three kids showed up a little while before the meal was ready.

Their son would always sit at the kitchen table and watch me cook. The poor little guy wasn't used to a home cooked meal. They usually ate a pizza, late at night, brought home by their dad. One time, though, I can't remember why I knew I had some extra work to do so I bought some noodles at the grocery store. They were dried in a bag and supposed to be homemade. But then when we started to eat the first thing my four-year-old did was take a bite of noodles. Then she looked at me and said "mama I know I'm eating something because I feel it in my mouth but I don't taste anything." I explained everything to her and told her I would make the noodles from then on.

CHAPTER 28

My first husband was a control freak like my mom. That's what my therapist told me when my doctor insisted I go to therapy. She said you married your mother. When I asked why, she said that's all you knew.

He was abusive in every way. The first time he shook me and threatened to kill me we had only been married six months. When I started to pack my clothes he said, "where are you gonna go? Back to your mommy?"

I had alternatives but I was so shocked I couldn't think straight. Then through the years I kept thinking things would get better if I would act different or dress different. Then he even started making fun of my body when other people thought it looked great.

When I married him, I thought we would get along good because we had both had a bad childhood and we would understand each other. Wrong! Thinking something won't make it happen. I truly had jumped out of the frying pan into the fire. He was worse than Mom.

CHAPTER 29

And I guess I should tell about my wedding. My brother had brought me to Gravelton, and I was getting ready at my Grandma's. My brother and his sister were going to stand up with us. Someone was bringing her from the city where she and most of his family lived. But their car broke down so my soon to be husband had to go get her.

By the time they got back it was getting late, but I had called the preacher, who lived in a town about 25 miles away. But he said it didn't matter how late we got there. My brother looked sad all evening. He knew I was making a mistake by not marrying Bill.

Finally after we were married, it was almost time for the midnight show, back about forty miles and him and his sister wanted to go there in the town where I used to go to the movies. He didn't want to go to the movies. He held my arm real tight to show off, that I had married him. But one young man came up to kiss the bride. Then he jerked me out of there.

When we started to go to the city, where he had rented the apartment and where his sister lived. She got in the backseat and went to sleep, in his old Studebaker with cardboard in one of the back windows.

Then when we got to a very dangerous city, we had to go through he decided he was too sleepy to drive and I would have to drive. I had never driven there before and I found out a few years later that the way he told me to go was the worst part of town. But he just told me which streets to go on, and got in the back seat with his sister and went to sleep.

When I drove down one street, there were drunk hoodlums standing in the edge of the street hollering at me to stop. They couldn't see the other two people in the back seat and they were both too sound asleep to hear what the men were saying or maybe they just didn't care.

So I drove through that city and 2 other little towns. When I got to the city where we were going to live I woke her up to show me where to take her. Then finally got him awake to show me the way to the apartment we were going to live in. I could tell it was not a very nice part of town. By the time we got there and carried everything upstairs, I was exhausted, but he was all rested, so you can guess what we did all day.

My brother was upset that I didn't marry Bill, but he didn't know I didn't think I was good enough.

CHAPTER 30

I spent an evening with two of my classmates after my divorce. If it hadn't been after my divorce it never would have happened. My ex had such a dirty mind it wouldn't have mattered that one was dying with cancer. The other was his best friend.

We had a nice time reminiscing about old times. Then one of them said, "you seem more like the person you should have always been." The other one agreed and I realized they were seeing the real person that I had never been allowed to be. I thanked them and thought maybe now I could just be me. And it really felt good. I didn't have to be someone's unwanted daughter, misunderstood sister or slave to do as I'm told.

I am a mother, grandmother, and great grandmother. These are the roles I love. But most of all I'm me.

CHAPTER 31

I SHOULD HAVE KNOWN MORE ABOUT my first husband before I married him but I really thought it would work. That was before I knew how lazy he was and what a pervert he was. In school I could be talking to some friends turn around and run right into him just standing there. Really! I'm surprised I didn't feel his hot breath on the back of my neck. And he was so lazy I had to dig out drains and ditches and help roof or he wouldn't do it.

CHAPTER 32

Back to when my dad had again been out of work and he would take any job to support his family. He found work in Hammond Indiana. I was 16 and had just finished my junior year of high school. I didn't know why at the time but mom wasn't as controlling when we moved there. She let me walk around with kids I had just met Ann, Joe and Al. One night we were walking around in the city when a new red Ford stopped. The young man driving asked if we wanted to ride around with him. Joe and Al knew him so they said sure. Ann and Al got in the backseat. Joe and I got in the front.

The young man drove to a drive-in restaurant and told us to order whatever we wanted. His name was Bill. While we were sitting there talking Bill looked at me and said "you have the most beautiful green eyes I've ever seen." Joe didn't like it and said "hey, she's with me." Bill just smiled and I think I said something about having my dad's eyes.

We rode around for a while then Bill took us all home. He took the boys home first. Then Ann and me. Ann lived next-door to us. After Ann walked away Bill asked me out. Of course I said yes then was surprised when mom said I could go.

Bill never honked the horn. He always came to the door to get me. We dated all that summer and I was so happy with him. He let me drive his car and took me to meet his mother. She liked me instantly to and got out a box of pictures telling me to take what I wanted.

I was so bashful I only took three. Later I told Bill I would have liked to take his graduation picture. He said I should have that his mom would give me anything. It was like I was in another world. Their apartment was so nice while ours was really crummy.

It didn't bother Bill though. He would come right in. Then when he brought me home, he would walk me to the steps, lift me up on the bottom one, kiss me good night then wait till I walked up the steps to our apartment. I found out later that his dad was dead and his stepdad had already moved to Alabama where his mom was going soon. Also the apartment house was Bill's with their six room apartment downstairs and another one upstairs that was rented.

CHAPTER 33

When I was 37, my nephew and I dug the hole for a new septic tank and the ditch off of it, while my ex ran a borrowed backhoe. That was on a Sunday. The next day I came home from my janitor job, fixed supper then slipped on the loose dirt by the ditch and broke my knee.

I told my girls to get their dad. I told him I heard it break and asked him to take me to the hospital. He said "you don't know it's broke you're not no GD doctor. Try to walk on it." And he wouldn't take me till I tried to walk.

Then instead of bringing the truck to me, he picked me up by my waist leaning sideways and carried me over 100 feet with it dangling. Then in the hospital, since I didn't know a surgeon they called one who I found out later was an alcoholic. He must've been really drunk that day. My knee doesn't even look the same and I've always had trouble with it. One day my brother said "can't you straighten your knees?" I didn't know I wasn't until he said that.

CHAPTER 34

BILL WANTED ME TO GO to Alabama with him to take his mother there. He also wanted me to meet his grandmother who lived there. I told him I knew mom wouldn't let me. So I didn't even ask her.

Later I told mom and she said she would have let me go. Probably just another lie. Bill had taken some college classes and had an office job. He also managed two performers. One night he needed to talk to one of them. He was a piano player in a very swanky nightclub. Bill said he wouldn't leave me in the car even though I wasn't old enough to be in there. I had never seen anything like it except in the movies.

Bill just took my hand as we walked up to the little stage to talk to the piano player. I was very thin at the time but had a good shape. After Bill introduced me to the man, he looked me over and said "she sure is a tiny little thing." With no hesitation Bill said "it's not the quantity that counts it's the quality." I was so impressed. I had never had anyone stand up for me before.

Bill wanted me to go to school up there but I was afraid to go to a large school. Bill took me lots of places. One night we went to a young couple's house. Bill and the other guy moved the table over in the dining room so we could dance. I had learned to dance when I was 14. A man who had been an Arthur Murray dance instructor had moved back to town and taught a lot of us kids to dance and didn't charge us. The instructor told me I was a natural.

One other night Bill started to take me to Chicago. He wanted me to see the lights at night. But when we got to the state line he stopped and turned around. He said he couldn't take me to another state because of my age. Bill talked about us getting married a lot. He said we wouldn't have to live in his apartment. That he would buy us a house with a white picket fence. But I just couldn't imagine being married to him. I just couldn't get it in my mind how someone smart and good looking could want someone like me.

Mom had me so beat down I thought I wasn't good enough for Bill. When mom told me that she would have let me go to Alabama with him I realized she probably wanted me to get pregnant like she did. She had already told me that I didn't need to graduate. She said she didn't and I would probably just get married and have kids anyway.

CHAPTER 35

Back now to when I was a child. Before I started school, I was just allowed to run around the neighborhood with nothing to eat until supper unless my friend's mom would give me something. She never even checked on me. That's how I got molested. But I won't go into detail. Enough said!

But it was another story at supper time when it was time for daddy. She would step outside and yell my name. If I couldn't run fast enough and she had to call me again she would be waiting with the yardstick. I still remember how bad it hurt on my bare legs. Years later I heard her tell my cousin and his wife "I never whipped any of my kids. Maybe just a little love pat." She looked real mean at me as if to say don't you say a word. I just sat there still thinking how she never loved me and she just sat there and lied. Now I know she wasn't capable of love. She was mentally unbalanced just like her mother.

CHAPTER 36

Three weeks before daddy died, he had told his sister that mom was getting so much worse he was going to have her committed to a mental hospital. Years later a doctor told me she probably killed him. I thought the doctor meant all the abuse. But then now I wonder if daddy let it slip and she poisoned his food. He had been doing so well. Then all at once he was back in the hospital. He never came home. Maybe that's what the doctor meant when she said that.

CHAPTER 37

I WAS NINE YEARS OLD WHEN mom's mom died. Sometimes when mom would go to fix her something to eat she would let me go with her. I would go into grandma's bedroom and say "hi grandma". She would just look mean at me. Even as a child, I wondered how I could have thought she might speak to me next time. She never did. I didn't mean to bother her so I would just be real quiet and stand against the wall. So after she looked mean at me she would just act like I was invisible. I guess mom must have lied to her to about leaving daddy if she hadn't had me. At this age 9 was when I had learned to pin curl my own hair and I had a little barrette that I liked. Someone either mom or uncle had cut my hair real short and I thought it looked OK but it was just something else for mom to belittle me about. Another repetitive thing for her to say every time she saw me, "your hair never looks as good as it did when I fixed it." Torture. That's what she did and I couldn't stop her. And she said that to me no matter how good it looked the rest of my life.

I married a control freak because that was all I knew. And when he thought I was going to leave he said he would get the kids and if he didn't he said he would not pay support. He said he would quit his job and lay in jail. If I had just been brave enough to challenge him but when he threatened to kill me I believed him.

I lived 50 years in fear because I believed two liars. I tried to kill myself but I couldn't in front of God. So when I got the nerve to leave I told him to go ahead and kill me because if I had to live with him one more day I would go crazy. So I held my arm straight out at my sides and said, "go ahead and shoot me. I don't care." I wasted my life on two no good freaks. I couldn't get away from mom but I could have gotten away from him.

CHAPTER 38

I GOT OFF TRACK AGAIN. BACK to when mom died. She insisted on having open heart surgery even with other health problems. My brother had been through it and tried to warn her. She even told Zelphia "you don't know, I might outlive all of you." She was 87. What a weird thing to say. My second husband, Don, said he would pray for her when she was getting ready for the surgery. She said, "thanks Don" even though she didn't like him. So I asked her if she wanted me to pray for her. I took her hand and with my two sisters and my brother watching I prayed and she squeezed my hand so hard my rings dug in my fingers. She just had to hurt me again anywhere in anyway.

She came through the surgery but never completely regained consciousness. On the third day the nurses said, "sometimes it helps to sing to them" so I sang to her. God has given me songs so I sang one of them. Can you imagine the one she hated the most singing it to her?

CHAPTER 39

MOM AND MY HUSBAND WERE both control freaks so they naturally heated each other. And since they both wanted to control me, I felt like a large rubber band with them pulling me apart. But my ex was also a sexual pervert. He thought he was such a stud that I was lucky to have him and all he thought about was sex. He shook me and choked me many times and he always told me if I ever found another man he would kill him but he would kill me first. He would also say, "I own you and don't you ever forget it."

I am pretty sure the reason he thought I would have an affair was because he had more than once. It was just a freak coincidence that I met a young woman and got to know her well enough to see her pictures.

CHAPTER 40

How I met her was I stopped at her yard sale. I started to get back in the car when the Holy Ghost told me to pray for her. So I went back and told her what had happened and asked her if I could pray for her.

She fell in my arms and told me how she needed prayer. So I prayed for her and gave her my phone number. A few weeks later she called me from jail. She was in jail for nine months and she kept giving me names and numbers of her so-called friends she thought would visit her. None of them did. I was her only visitor and I became in charge of her property. That's how I saw her pictures.

I took two of her pictures to the jail and asked her where she got pictures of my daughter. Turned out the pictures weren't my daughter and the two pictures weren't even of the same girl. But they looked so much like my daughter that even she thought they were her. I personally think the girls belongs to my ex-husband but I'll probably never know for sure. Thing is, if they are my daughters half-sisters they need to know even though they are all grown up now. These were old pictures. So what happens now? I gave the pictures to my other daughter. It's up to them now. I told her to talk to her dad but don't know if she did.

I know they say everyone has a double but two in the same city 25 miles away? Too much of a coincidence. So this is the man who when I told him he owed our daughters respect said, "I don't owe them a GD thing!" And now I think how did I ever have two children with a man like that? My life as a soap opera? Right? And I might have already said this but who goes hunting or fishing and comes back with nothing and without any dirt on their clothes or shoes? I don't know why I thought things would get better. And why I didn't wonder where he had really been.

CHAPTER 41

I HAD AN EXPERIMENTAL SURGERY WHEN I was 21 because I had been told by my doctor, after testing, that I would never be able to have a baby. I knew I wanted babies and I thought he liked kids. But after the surgery the surgeon said that even if I did get pregnant which he thought wasn't possible that I'd never carry it full-term because my uterus was so small.

The surgery was called a wedge resection which involves cutting the ends of my closed tubes off. Then cutting a wedge from my ovaries and sewing my tubes to my ovaries. I almost died because back then in January 1963, they didn't give you glucose water and they didn't weigh you to adjust the anesthetic. They just gave me an adult dose when I should have had a child's dose. When I only weighed 110 pounds. I was unconscious for three days.

I also found out I had Hyperglycemia later when I passed out in the doctor's office. A nurse told me later that the nurses in that hospital saved my life by walking, well really dragging me, up and down the halls every two hours around the clock. I couldn't see. Everything was just a blur. And I was hallucinating.

I told them once that the pieces of my body were hanging on the wall above the fireplace. But the nurses we're so patient with me. They would put my arms around their shoulders and keep saying, "come on take a step." I was completely at their mercy but they did their jobs otherwise I would have gone in a coma and died or had brain damage.

I didn't eat anything until the third evening and with low blood sugar, them walking me kept my blood circulating and me alive. The third evening one of the nurses said, "can't you think of anything you can eat?"

I told her maybe an orange. She said if the cafeteria doesn't have one I'll get in my car and go to the store and get you one.

I was so close to dying she was willing to do anything. She came back with an orange but someone had to peel it for me and feed it to me because I couldn't see it. After I ate the orange and some crackers, my vision started to return and I started to wake up. It took me so long to recuperate though and I never regained the boundless energy I had before.

Years later, I was diagnosed with fibromyalgia and chronic fatigue. Then I went to a seminar and the main doctor said he couldn't prove it but he knew that trauma caused it. He invited people to ask questions and when I told him about my surgery he said he had no doubt that had caused it.

CHAPTER 42

About two years later though I did get pregnant but when I was about seven months my exes brother had a party and my ex got so drunk I almost had to carry him in the house. Then he laid down on the couch and threw up all over the couch and floor. When I started cleaning it up he said, "you can't clean that up. You are pregnant." If he knew I was pregnant then he knew he was vomiting. He just didn't care where he did it.

CHAPTER 43

Then when I was almost 8 months along mom came to stay. She said she thought I would go early and she wanted to be there. In all reality, she just hadn't been able to torture me for a while. She and my first hated each other so bad that the next three weeks were really miserable.

She nagged me all day every day then him half the night. He wanted to make her leave but I was so afraid that if he told her to and they fought I wouldn't be able to stand it. Finally one night my dad called. He said he was sick and wanted her to come home. I still wasn't to my due date so I told her to go on home. She got so mad and said, "you always thought more of him than me. He's probably not even sick." Later when I thought about it I thought he probably just thought I couldn't stand anymore and that could have just been his way of protecting me like he always did when I was a little kid.

CHAPTER 44

Anyway she wasn't there when I had my baby. But I was so stressed my baby wouldn't drop. It was August and with no air-conditioning the last six weeks the only way I could sleep was with a box fan on a kitchen chair right in my face while propped up in a sitting position. I started having contractions on a Saturday morning.

So all day I cleaned my house, I mopped and waxed on my hands and knees, swept all the rugs with a broom (no sweeper), dusted, scrubbed everything till the house was spotless. Sunday morning the pains got closer. In the hospital, I had to walk down a long haul to the bathroom. I didn't know anything about having a baby so I thought what if I have it in the stool? Fat chance!

That evening when the nurses thought I was ready I was in the delivery room a few more hours. My doctor was walking the halls like any normal expectant dad would do but not my lazy ex. He was probably asleep somewhere. His mom said when he called her he said, "mom Rhoda had her baby." The nurse was trying to help me get the baby worked down telling me when to push finally I said, "I'm sorry! I can't push any harder" I was taking the blame as usual. But that sweet little redheaded nurse said, "oh! Honey it's not your fault. This baby is just stubborn."

My doctor even came in the room and said, "we are the ones that feel sorry for you." I am sure all that stress from mom and my ex caused me not to be able to relax but who am I kidding? I don't remember one time in my life that I've ever been totally relaxed. Thanks a lot! To the people who were supposed to love me not control me. There's an old country song that says you wanted a fool and I played the part. That's how I feel but I know God lives in me so I am OK.

CHAPTER 45

Anyway when we got the baby worked down a little bit that sweet little nurse got up on the gurney on her knees right beside me. She put both arms across my upper stomach and ribs. She said, "when you go to sleep I'm going to do your pushing for you. The next thing I remember was waking up saying, "this is my baby! She's really my baby! She's really mine!" The baby's head was so big the newborn bonnet fit her. That's why I had so many stitches.

I was in the hospital five days. In the car and after I got home, I couldn't sit flat for three weeks. But just to show you what kind of a freak I was married to when he drove me home he came around the car took the baby out of my arms and walked in the house. He just left me sitting there. Sweet guy right?

CHAPTER 46

I GUESS THE THERAPIST WAS RIGHT. He was just like mom. Just look out for number one.

CHAPTER 47

But for years I never argued with him or my mom. Many years later when I finally stood up for myself he said, "what happened to you? You're nothing like you used to be." I said, "thank God! I finally woke up." Even though I married him, he was so jealous and insecure he thought I wouldn't stay. The only reason I did stay was because I was so afraid of him. I really believed he would kill me.

One of his cousins felt sorry for him and said he couldn't stand to lose his wife. I told her, "he didn't lose me he drove me away." Other people said they never seen such big old tears when he cried in the taverns. But no one knew how I had cried for years. I didn't want the world to know, so I cried my tears at home.

But the day I left I told him to take one of the two guns he carried in each front pocket (one was mine he took away from me) and go ahead and shoot me I don't care anymore. He said, "you're crazy just like the rest of your GD family." I said. "I must be to stay with you all these years." Then he said; "you're going to find another man ain't you?" I said, "the last thing in this world I want is another man if they are all like you."

Before I left though he had left and was gone all weekend. I had no idea where he was but thought he might come back in the night to kill me. So I hid those two nights lying on the floor behind a rack of clothes in one of the rooms I hadn't finished. Didn't get much sleep.

When he came back on Monday I told him Rebecca had been out looking for him all weekend. She thought he might have had a wreck and been unconscious or dead. I told him he should have had enough respect to tell his daughters where he was that he owed them that much respect. He said, "I don't owe them a GD thing."

CHAPTER 48

Back to mom and that formal living room. Besides one neighbor woman, I only remember one couple visiting in that room. They were people they had known as kids who were visiting relatives and stopped by for a little while. And for that my brother had to grow up without a bedroom.

I probably embarrassed mom then by selling them my last three little sacks of walnuts. I had been picking them up and hulling them with a hammer. One day daddy saw me so he jacked the car up and had me throw them under one wheel. It was sure a lot faster that way but I'm sure mom didn't like it because he was paying attention to me. I was real little at that time but I would try to mow the yard with daddy's push mower after I picked up all the walnuts so he wouldn't have to do it after work. But I was just too little.

Back to that couple, he made some silly remark that made mom think she could have married him. She always thought she could have done better than daddy. But in all reality daddy could have done better than her. Anyone would have been better than her.

The pictures my aunt would take were really something. My dad would stand humbly but she would always pose like she thought she was a model. You know look at me!

CHAPTER 49

I REMEMBER ONCE WHEN SHE WAS repeating that same old lie about daddy. I said, "why didn't you leave when you got me in school?" She screamed at me, "it was too late then. My life was over." She was 29 and lived to be 87. Not quite over right?

My mom and my ex-husband were alike in another way. They were never wrong. And they never said they were sorry. Of course not. Everything was my fault. My ex-husband even said he was fat because I cooked too much. No one forced him to eat so much.

One time there was a house for sale in our town and my brother told me to bid on it for him which I did. Then my ex-husband bid more. The real estate agent said, "you're bidding against your wife." He told him he didn't care. But my brother had already borrowed the money from his credit union. My ex only wanted it because my brother did. He was jealous of everyone. But I gave in again. We were living in it when we split up. My ex never spent one night in it but wouldn't let me live in it.

He also wouldn't pay the insurance on his truck. Since the truck and the car I drove were billed together he thought I would pay it. The insurance agent wouldn't separate them so I was forced to file for divorce. He counter-sued and he and his lawyer drug it out for 18 months.

CHAPTER 50

During this time, I was supposed to pay the house payment on the house we had moved out of in the country and my ex was supposed to pay the payment on the one in town which my brother had the loan. But he wouldn't pay it. I found out when my brother finally told me he had been making the payments.

Then when the divorce was final and they auctioned both the houses my ex got the bid on the house in Town and was supposed to have the money within 30 days. He didn't get the money for three months. My brother could have taken the house but he didn't. He was just too good. If there is such a thing as being too good, my brother was the epitome of that. I'll tell you more about him later.

CHAPTER 51

Back to when I was 16, my brother and I went to Gravelton for the weekend after school had been going for eight weeks. Mom had said I didn't need to graduate. But while we were in Gravelton, my friends talked me into staying. We didn't have a phone so I called the people in the downstairs apartment and asked them to get my dad on the phone.

He wanted me to graduate so I knew he would say yes and I knew I could catch up on the eight weeks of school. Dad never told me about the hell he went through with mom for letting me stay. That's probably what caused his next heart attack.

But now back to my brother. He was going with a girl when he joined the Marines. She promised to wait for him. She was still in school about three years younger than Dan. As far as we knew she was still planning to marry him. They wrote back-and-forth and he sent her gifts all the time.

But all that time she was dating some rich man. She didn't tell my brother until he came home. Danny was devastated and started drinking all the time. I was so mad at her and told my brother it was her fault. He told me not to be mad at her. He said "maybe someday I'll find a cute little girl with a big nose like you." He did but before that something else happened.

CHAPTER 52

Sounds like a soap opera but just wait. After I graduated, I took a friend back to Hammond with me and we both got a restaurant job. Eventually she got pregnant with my brother's son. Just something else mom blamed on me. Blame game. And I did feel quite guilty but mom said she could stay with us.

My brother bought rings and they were planning their wedding. But three troublemakers from our town traveled all those miles and told my brother that the baby wasn't his. He shouldn't have listened to them and meant to just put the wedding off for a while but that didn't work out either. By this time, I had married my first husband. Big mistake! But I just couldn't admit it.

My brother paid support and gave the baby his name. He planned to go talk to his son when he was 18 but his son was killed at 17. My brother was always sorry that he didn't marry my friend but to this day she calls me her sister-in-law. Things just didn't seem to work out for Dan or me but it was messes of our own making.

My brother eventually did find a girl with a big nose like me but that was another mistake. How could he have known that she would run with other men and years later brag about it? The two kids she had are both drug addicts, been in prison and just made Danny miserable. The second one isn't Danny's because he told me and told her. One is back in prison now. Who knows who the kids belong to? They don't look anything like my brother. The boy my friend had did look like him.

CHAPTER 53

Now back to my life. If I am supposed to be so smart, how could I have kept thinking things would get better if I did this or that? Or acted different in some way. They only got worse. Until the day I just couldn't take anymore. I thought about killing myself. Even went to the woods with a gun three times. But how could I do that with God watching? God didn't like divorce so I wondered if he would still love me if I got a divorce. I felt like that rubber band again. Just being stretched to my limit. The day I left my ex though I stood outside with my arms stretched out and said, "go ahead and shoot me."

CHAPTER 54

BEFORE THE GIRLS GREW UP, he had told me many times that he would get them because he had the good job to support them and if he didn't get them, he would not pay support. He said he would quit his job and lay in jail. And he probably would have enjoyed it since he was so lazy.

He carried a small gun in each front pocket that he planned to use to kill me. He said he would say he didn't remember what happened but I started to wonder if he thought his lies might not hold up. Something else he lied about, he said he would never let anyone say anything vulgar or smart to me or our daughters. But my youngest had already told me that a man said something vulgar to her when she was with her dad and he had said nothing.

Anyway, I had worked the all night shift. The manager came in to start his shift at 6 o'clock. The weasel had been asleep in the office laying on the big desk. I was getting ready to count my drawer money when the man from town came in, he wanted to know if I remembered a time when Dory and I stripped for him. I looked at my ex. He said nothing. I told the man he knew that wasn't true. And that Dory or me weren't that kind of people. Then I said, "anyway if I was going to strip for anyone it sure as hell wouldn't have been you." His face turned red and he couldn't get out of the door fast enough. In a way I think I unleashed my pent up anger on the man who said something bad about my friend Dory and me. I didn't even think I could talk that way. I surprised myself.

CHAPTER 55

During the 18 months when I was waiting for the divorce to be final, I was virtually homeless. My brother and his second wife had a teeny tiny house. I would go there after work and take a shower. Then I would stay as long as I could before going to my younger sister's trailer to sleep on her couch. She was the only other one who had room for me. But the reason I tried to wait as long as I could was because my mom had gradually moved in with sis and her husband so she could take over their lives.

A control freak always has to have someone to control. But no matter how late I waited, mom was always waiting for me. She would start right in on me. Telling me I couldn't use the bathroom because I might wake them. I would just lay down on the couch with my back to my mom and pretend to sleep. During these long months I did any kind of work I could get with my clothes and tools in an old car with a rod knocking. I would work long hours double shifts and for lots of old people who trusted me because I was a woman.

CHAPTER 56

One thing I forgot one time before daddy died, I walked up on my parent's porch and heard her lying to daddy about me. So I knew then that she was trying to turn him against me. She told him that I had scolded Rebecca for something and not Rachel for the same thing. She had been at my house earlier that day sitting at my table at one end of my long kitchen. I was cooking supper at the other end. I hadn't seen Rachel doing it. I told her that and also that if she saw her she should have said something. But no! Anything to make me look bad.

CHAPTER 57

Another story about my mom. Someone shot my brother's dog. We never knew who did it and my parents never tried to remove the bullets from his hip. Consequently, he lived the rest of his life with it under the skin in the muscle of his right hip. After that happened, he became extremely gun shy.

In the summer when the screen doors were being used and it would start storming, he was so afraid he would tear through the screen to get in the house and hide under the bed. Then mom would get the broom and hit him till she got him outside. I never understood why she did this. It would have been much better to just let him in until the storm was over.

He was a good dog and wouldn't have hurt anything. But she was the boss and liked to gripe about him tearing the screen over and over and over. One time he had followed us to school when it started to storm and some kids let him in. He got in the girl's basement bathroom.

I had to go upstairs to get my brother to make his dog go out into the storm. My brother looked so sad. I just thought of another thing, early this morning while not sleeping around 5 o'clock. I hadn't been married very long when the weasel got laid off from his job. At least that's what he said so we went back to Gravelton and stayed with his mom.

That's when I first saw how lazy he was. His brother and his wife and child were also there. Their mother picked up two five gallon buckets to go out to get coal while the weasel and his brother laid on her two couches. I said, "are you two going to lay there and let your mother carry in the coal?" They didn't even budge. I told them I couldn't believe they would let their mother carry the coal to warm their lazy butts. Then I went out to help her. I should have just left and not gone back.

CHAPTER 58

A FEW DAYS LATER, MY SISTER Zelphia who lived about 20 miles away called the neighbor asking for me. My mother-in-law didn't have a phone. She said she was sick and asked if I could come help her. So I had the weasel take me to her house. He came in with me and I wouldn't let him leave until he took her to the doctor. She looked like she was dying. She couldn't even get her lips to cover her teeth her face was so drawn.

I had to put her coat on her and instruct the weasel to help her to the car and into the doctor. While I stayed with the baby she had just had and her five-year-old. She had to be in bed and given medicine and fed. The baby had to be fed by pumping his jaws to get the formula in. Then I had to weigh him after each feeding and if he lost a half an ounce I had to call his doctor. I also had to fix supper for Zelphia's husband who the first evening said, "what are you doing here?" Zelphia very adamantly instructed me not to call mom but the third day I was there the crazy uncle came after he dropped his school teacher wife off at school.

I was doing a good job and the baby and Zelphia were improving but he went back to the school, got my aunt and dropped her off then drove straight to Hammond to get my mom. I was read the riot act by everybody for not calling mom but I told them all that Zelphia didn't want her there. Well the next morning mom told me to leave and she told everybody that she and little sis saved Zelphia and the babies lives when the truth is they were well on the way to recovery before she even got there. Just another lie.

CHAPTER 59

Zelphia played the piano. Our cousin, Ivy, had taken lessons and taught Zelphia how to chord so she would pick out the melodies to lots of songs. I would sit on the piano stool with her and we would sing together. She would sing the harmony and I would sing the melody. That was before she got married. Then after she had been married a little while her husband got drafted and she moved back home so we got to sing together again and she got better and better on the piano.

CHAPTER 60

THE EX WAS SO LAZY that when he was let go from a job his cousin had gotten for him and exhausted all his unemployment even going so far as to take welding classes. We had to buy books and new welding hats every week but as soon as he cashed his last check he never went back to school. One day another man that worked where he worked later said, "well I wouldn't call it work. He slept on the fork truck most of the night."

I was working two jobs and babysitting. But he didn't care then when he finally got a job on the days, I didn't have to work the second job. I got off at six. Had to read the pumps, stick the tanks, count my drawer, enter the numbers in the books and drive home. But the phone would be ringing before I could get the key in the door.

When I answered he would say, "where in the hell have you been?" I worked in another town but in that half hour the weasel thought I had time to have an affair. He even called my boss' wife and told her he was having an affair with me.

My boss told me about it but didn't fire me. I guess they knew he was crazy. Here's another story I almost forgot. Someone gave us a window unit air conditioner. We had never had one before. The girls loved it. They were about eight and ten.

One very hot evening the weasel came in the door with a man from town and said, "I gave him that air conditioner." My girls were lying on the floor enjoying the cool air watching television. I said, "why would you do that?" He said in a grouchy tone, "because we don't need it." The man could see I was really upset when I started to cry and he said, "I won't take it if you don't want me to." I said through tears, "what am I supposed to say? He said he already gave it to you." Then they unplugged it and took it out of the window with my girls and I all crying.

CHAPTER 61

I NEVER THOUGHT MUCH OF THAT man after that. I think the weasel was just so in love with himself he wanted people to think I would stay with him even though we had to do without things we needed. His cousin, who was a sweet man, even smarted off to him when he found out we didn't have a microwave. He said what the hell is wrong with you? You should get her the things she needs. But the weasel just shrugged his shoulders, only cared about himself and what he wanted.

I think he really worshipped his own body. He also made fun of my body saying my butt was too big and my neck was too long. But he hardly had a neck. He was like the kids in that well-known movie where someone called the kids little no neck bastards. I won't name the movie but some people will remember. I think he made fun of my body because other people would say how good I looked.

One person even said I could have been a high fashion model. And when his sisters kept saying I was too skinny one sister's boyfriend said, "I'm getting tired of hearing that. She is not skinny. She has a good shape. She's just thin." I'll come back to this but right now I want to go back to before I was married.

Back to that childless couple in town. She was a piano teacher and I had begged mom to let me take lessons but she said we couldn't afford them. They were just $.50. Our cousin, who had taken lessons, showed my older sister how to chord and she went on from there and got pretty good.

Every time I went over to the piano to pick out something mom would come in there and tell me to get up and let her play. She knew two or three little ditties was all but she didn't want me to have enough time to learn. I know I'm getting off track here but I want to tell this.

One time after Zelphia had remarried she had a real nice piano. Mom and my other sister were going to visit her. She told me she had practiced some songs and was just waiting for them to ask her to play. But, oh no, she said mom just sat down at the piano and did the very little bit she knew. Then got up and said well it's got a pretty good tone.

Zelphia said it hurt her feelings so bad. But she should have been used to it. Oh and something else I might as well say here. We three older kids all married control freaks like mom and they all ran around on us and had kids with other people and all three marriages ended in divorce. Now back to where I got off track.

The man was the superintendent of the schools. One day when we were in the first grade he came in our room. Our teacher told us we were going to have a play called the Tom Thumb wedding. Then the man came over and picked me up and said, "and you're going to be the bride."

The mothers of some of the kids made all the costumes and decided all the girls should have their hair in long curls. Of course, my mom never agreed with anyone about anything so she said my hair wouldn't go in long curls. This was a lie because sometimes when I curl it it falls in long curls on my shoulders. Anyway, since mom wouldn't go in there the other mothers jerked me around and tried to make my hair go in long curls. I still remember them hurting me and I'm sure I went on stage crying. All because mom didn't think enough of me to go in the room to dress me. But anyway they had my hair messed up so grandma, daddy's mom, was so mad she made the photographer wait while she tried to fluff up my hair. She was a tall woman so she just stood in front of the stage to do this. I can still remember the whole thing. I didn't know what an honor it was to be the bride. I just wondered why my dress was white and the other girls had pretty colored dresses.

Then in third grade my two cousins and I wore the dresses to sing at an older cousins wedding. We sang I love you truly. Back to the play when the women got us back in our own clothes the women took the little padlock ring from my finger and gave it to the little boy's mom who played the groom. I have it now because she gave it to me years later. But if I had of had it then mom would have gotten rid of it like she did some of my other stuff. Or what she did keep she gave to my younger sister. Then when I asked her about things she would deny ever knowing about them. Some things I had bought with my own money that other people gave me.

Born with a broken heart and then blamed for crying

My grandma's house in the country where I used to stay with her burned and my aunt built a four-room house there. Later we bought it from my aunt and built on to it. The weasel was working at a job that his cousin got for him and he started carrying a lunch bucket so he could steal the nails for the addition. I tried to talk him out of it saying why would you want your daughters living in a house built with stolen nails and anyway they're not that expensive? We built on too much anyway. He always had to act important. We ended up with a 10-room house and two wood stoves and me carrying the wood.

He also insisted on bulldozing the hill behind it. I told him it would be to steep and he would never get grass to grow. He wouldn't listen. So he bulldozed grandma's root cellar and the pretty Ivy she had growing there and ended up mowing little twigs of grass and dirt with his many mowers. While I carried the wood. The only time he helped was if someone came to visit or the girls came home. Anyone with half a brain could tell I had been caring the wood with my hair wet from the rain or snow. But he'd jump up in a stupor and say, "oh, I'll get that."

Also if we were splitting wood, he ran the lever and I lifted the wood to be split but I had to keep my daughters warm. When he insisted on the bulldozing and I couldn't change his mind it took all the money I had saved to do it. Then every time it rained the rain would pour down the hill and into the house across the cement slab floor. I dug a trench behind the cement slab so many times I can't remember but it would just fill with mud then go across the floor every time. The weasel would just keep throwing grass seed on the hill which was washed down with the mud into the ditch I dug over and over.

He was such a know it all he just kept mowing little twigs of weeds and kept buying mowers with the money I saved. All he cared about was people saw him mowing. I wondered if they saw he was just throwing dirt instead of grass. I mowed with a push mower around the house and eventually the rain washing in over the slab ruined the carpet. I just couldn't keep up. Another thing when we lived there his cousin asked him to tear a room off their garage. The wood was still good but had huge nails in it. Anyway we brought it home and I thought he was going to help me pull the nails and use the lumber to screen in our back porch. He said you can do it but don't ask me to help you. I did it all myself and the neighbor

Man told me he was glad I didn't work where he did because they would expect everyone to work as hard as I did. Anyway when I got it all done and the porch swing up the weasel sat out there every morning and drank his coffee. He had no shame.

CHAPTER 62

Another story, when I was about 12 mom pointed to a little drawer in her nightstand and said there's some things in there you're going to need some day and that's all she said. I had no idea what she was talking about. Then one day I was home alone and when I went to the outside toilet there was blood on the crumpled up catalog pages we used as toilet paper. I was so scared. I just walked back in the house wondering what was wrong with me. She wasn't home but I thought maybe that was what she had been talking about. In the drawer. I found some thick things with ends and an elastic thing with two metal things. I figured out how to use them. This was my introduction to womanhood.

CHAPTER 63

Now back to my life. If I am supposed to be so smart how could I have kept thinking things would get better if I did this or that or if I acted different in some way. Or if I dressed different. After the kids grew up, I was still trying to stay but things got worse when he didn't have to act nice for anyone anymore. I was so unhappy I thought about killing myself. I even went to the woods with a gun three times. I would look up at the sky and think how can I do this with God watching me? So I would go back to the house and dance to the radio by myself.

CHAPTER 64

The day I left my ex for good he said again I should kill you. I stood outside with my arms stretched out and told him go ahead and shoot me. Take that gun out of your pocket and shoot me. I don't care anymore. He had always told me that he would get my daughters and if he didn't he wouldn't pay support. But they were grown now. There was no reason to stay. He carried a small gun in each front pocket and a 357 under the seat in his truck. Who needs that many guns? Just a coward. I had to take care of everything that happened with my girls and myself. He always said he could kill me and never spend a day in jail. When it came right down to it maybe he knew his lies wouldn't hold up.

CHAPTER 65

Here's something else he lied about. He said he would never let anyone talk vulgar or mean to me or my daughters. But my youngest had told me that a man had said something really vulgar to her in front of her dad and he didn't say a word. Then when a man said something vulgar to me right in front of him he sat there and didn't say a word. I looked over at him and then took care of it myself. I sent the man out of the establishment where I work with a red face. The man was a creep and we both knew what he said wasn't true but the man didn't expect to be talked to the way I talk to him. I had work the all night shift while the weasel slept in the back room. I was tired and I knew I had to babysit in just a few hours. I needed to sleep before that happened. Then when we got in the car the weasel started cussing the man. So I said, "hey you sat there like a lily livered coward when you knew he was lying. You let me take care of it myself. So don't cuss him now I need to rest before I have to babysit." The man had said that Dory and I stripped for him. I said "you know that's not true." I was so mad I said, "if I was going to strip for anyone it sure as hell wouldn't have been you."

CHAPTER 66

My friend Dory went to Hammond with me for spring break when we were seniors. She and I had walked to a big grocery store. That's where we saw Bill. He was so glad to see me. He said he needed to go home and clean up. I had never seen him unshaven. He said, "will you call me in a little while? It won't take me long. We can go somewhere." When we got back to my parent's apartment she said come on let's go call him. When I didn't get up she said' "if you don't call him you're crazy." I said. "but I'm going with someone." She said. "I don't care, call Bill."

When I still didn't get up she said again/ "you're crazy." If only I had listened to her. But I was being loyal to the weasel even before we were married. If only I had listened to Dory I would have married Bill. Later I figured out that God had brought Bill and I back together. But by the time I finally got it, it was too late. I was so sorry I hadn't called him biggest mistake of my life! And I knew I had hurt Bill's feelings. I even tried to find him years later to tell him how sorry I was. But I never could find him. If I ever get this book published maybe he'll read it and know how very sorry I still am. I really thought I wasn't good enough for Bill. I've never felt the same about anyone but Bill but my mom had me so beat down I thought I was lower than dirt. I ended up marrying the weasel and he sure wasn't loyal to me ever. He started mistreating me when we hadn't been married very long. While he made fun of my body he was always bragging on his own. I could never say the things he said about his own body. They were too gross. It became really obvious he really loved himself. He was a hopeless narcissist. He loves himself so much he has no love left for anyone else.

CHAPTER 67

I MUST GET ON ANOTHER SUBJECT. I need to tell everyone about my cousin Judy. She is 15 months younger than me. Her dad retired from the Navy as a lieutenant commander. He told us kids that he had begged my dad to join with him. He said, "your dad was so much smarter than me he would have been an admiral." Anyway Judy and I were so close that no matter how long they were gone when they came back it was like we'd never been apart. There was only one thing Judy did that I didn't like. There was always old, mangy dogs in town. Judy would pet them. Now I love dogs. I don't ever want to be without dogs in my life, I just don't want to pet mangy ones.

CHAPTER 68

WE WOULD ALWAYS STAY AT grandmas and spend most of the night fluffing the featherbed. We would take turns being the first to jump in it. It would be so fluffy it would almost envelop the first one. Sometimes if we giggled too loud Pa would holler, "you girls settled down up there." They slept downstairs. Everyone loved to stay at grandmas. When she called everyone for breakfast it was a feast. Bacon, sausage, fried potatoes, gravy, biscuits, homemade apple butter, and jelly. But the eggs were the most fascinating part. She would just fry a big iron skillet full of probably two dozen. If there were a lot of us there. Then she would pile them all on a big plate and you just took as many as you wanted when it was passed around. Oh! And none of the yolks were ever broken. Grandma was such a wonderful woman. One of a kind. Grandpa would drink too much but she wouldn't cuss him. She would just say. "you old bird."

CHAPTER 69

Here's another story about grandma. Pa's dad had moved from his nice brick home in the country to a little shotgun house between us and grandma before he got too old and had to be put in a nursing home. Anyway grandma, not Pa, would visit him every Saturday and she always took me with her. The old people were so sad but grandma would just visit every patient. It was just an old house in the country but I don't think some of the patients had any other visitors. We didn't see anyone else there and the old people always wanted to touch me or my hair. I was probably only about four and it scared me at first but grandma would put her arms around me to let me know it was OK. They all appreciated grandma so much and would always say, "please come back and bring your pretty little girl with you." Then I would spend the night with grandma she would curl my hair on the tops from coffee sacks. That's what women used for curlers. I love staying with grandma. She was so different than mom. She would put her arms around me and let me snuggle up to her something that my mom never did. We would look at her picture album and sing church songs. I couldn't read yet but I knew the words from going to church with her since I was probably three. She was the one who made sure I knew about Jesus and she must have suspected how bad mom treated me because although she had lots of grandkids she always seem to take a special interest in me.

CHAPTER 70

Another thing about great grandpa when he lived in a little shotgun house I would go sit on his little stoop which only had room for his one chair. He would smoke his pipe and tell me about growing up in Kentucky on his parent's farm where he was always barefoot.

CHAPTER 71

Back now to my first husband. We moved so many times. Every time I got a place fixed up he was ready to move. He knew the people who owned the crummy places would give us two or more free month's rent for me cleaning their dumps up. I even cleaned up maggots in one house but when I finished it you couldn't even tell it was the same house. The weasel thought he was outsmarting me but I liked that kind of work. Well not the maggots.

CHAPTER 72

Then through the years I kept thinking things would get better. When I married him I thought we would get along well because we both had bad childhoods. But he was a control freak just like mom. Of course, I didn't know that until many years later when my doctor insisted I go to therapy. It took almost 2 years for me to know why I did what I did and why my older sister and brother did the same thing. What it all boils down to is we all three married our mother because that's all we knew. The simple way to say it is we jumped out of the frying pan into the fire. I knew the weasel was jealous but I thought when I married him he wouldn't be. Boy was I wrong. When I was in high school, I could be talking to some friends turn around and run right into him just standing there. Really! Later when I figured out what a pervert he was and thought it over I'm surprised I didn't feel his hot breath on the back of my neck.

CHAPTER 73

One time when we went to the funeral home for a visitation for a man's wife who had died in a car wreck and his young daughter was still in the hospital. I hugged him and told him I was sorry. Then I asked about his daughter and his knees buckled as he started to fall. So I caught him and steadied him till he composed himself. My ex didn't say a word until we got in the car. Then he said it was bad enough that you hugged him once did you have to hug him twice? I said I caught him when he started to fall. Why didn't you help? But he just cussed.

CHAPTER 74

When we moved back to Gravelton and made friends the woman's parents had been friends with my exes parents when they were kids. One time when we were at the friend's house her sister came in and ran right over to my ex and kissed him telling him how glad she was to see him after probably 15 years. My ex acted OK till we got home. Then he said, "are you mad?" I said, "about what?" He said, "she kissed me. You should be mad and jealous." Then he got really mad because I wasn't. I knew she was just glad to see him but he took it wrong because of the way his mind worked. Everything to him was about sex.

CHAPTER 75

Another thing one time he told me he wanted to screw me in every room in the house. Who would want to screw in their young innocent daughter's bedrooms? To me it was like a dog who runs around marking everything by peeing on it.

CHAPTER 76

In 2008 my daughter was trying out for a musical play. I tried out with her and made it at 67. It was fun. I hadn't been in a play since my junior and senior class plays. In both of those I was the teenage daughter and in one, my good friend, had to pretend he was kissing me. The audience loved it. He let me drive his car once but never asked me out. He liked girls with big boobs which I didn't have. But we were close friends. I had lots of close friends including boys which my ex could never understand. To him it was about sex. And he thought every boy wanted to screw me. He thought that way so he thought everyone did.

CHAPTER 77

During the time I was homeless I got to know the man who wanted to help me. When he found out I was in the hospital after I had had a nervous breakdown he told the nurses what was going on. He asked if he could sleep there because he thought my ex might come in there to hurt me. So the nurses would bring in a little fold up cot at night and wake him each morning to go to work. He also had my sis to be there while he was at work. Mom came to but for once she didn't nag me or if she did I didn't know it because I was knocked out all the time. They did wake me long enough for me to be taken to my lawyer's office to sign a restraining order. Then the little cowardly weasel took out one on me. What a joke! And someone instructed the switchboard operators to not let any calls through that didn't know the code. This was before hospitals did things like that. At least I got some much-needed rest. Now the control freaks didn't stop though. Mom told a story about me hiding under a desk and the weasel called my doctor and told someone there that I was faking everything. I just slept through it all.

CHAPTER 78

Mom and sis insisted on taking me to the courthouse but I wouldn't let them go in. When I came out the man I'll call Don was there too. By this time he knew a lot about what was happening. Everything went for the weasel. I was even ordered to give the weasel things that I had saved and paid for. I think that was because the judge and the weasel's lawyer were friends. Also the judge had been the sheriff when the weasel was a kid and when people would call the sheriff about his dad he would threaten to kill the sheriff so he wouldn't arrest him. So I did what the judge said because I didn't want to go to jail and besides I don't look good in orange. At least I was free, but I was still scared because the weasel was still driving past the house all night. When I told Don he loaned me a shotgun. He said even if I did know how to shoot if the weasel broke in the best thing for me to have would be a shotgun. So I had a phone put in and a stool in the bathroom. The floor had caved in so the stool couldn't be used so I had to have the floor fixed too. Up until then I had used a bucket. But anything was better than listening to mom half the night. I hadn't been sleeping well never did really so I watch the weasel drive past the house till daylight. I was down to 98 pounds too from all the stress. I have a poem I wrote about my ex called the weasel in disguise I am going to include it in this book.

CHAPTER 79

When I finally found a house in another town I was so happy even though I still had to go to my brothers to take a shower. I also had to carry milk jugs of water to flush the stool. The house had an old well with a pump but it hadn't been used for so many years. I just waited till I could save the money to have city water put in. It took nine months. My brother kept trying to help me but he wasn't in good health after his open-heart surgery. He had enough problems with his kids (one didn't even belong to him) stealing from him, to sell his stuff for their drugs. They also expected him to support them and their kids. I didn't want to add to his stress so I told him I was OK.

CHAPTER 80

My brother and I were so close that I knew when something was wrong with him. When he had his second heart attack I had been up all night waiting for the phone to ring. I was still with the weasel at that time and I had a hysterectomy one month before. I had been having trouble for a year or more and when a DNC didn't help the doctor said my hemoglobin was dropping too much. I started hemorrhaging so bad it was like turning on a faucet. The weasel saw me bleeding that bad when he opened the shower door. When I got out of the shower I had to put a beach towel between my legs then wash the blood off my legs then I had to go to the hospital for the doctor to check me out. The doctor gave me a prescription for pills they give women after they have a baby and hemorrhage. The doctor threw the beach towel in the trash put three pads on me and sent me to the pharmacy. Now you might think the weasel would go in and get the meds for me but no I had to walk to the back of the pharmacy. Then they didn't have the meds I needed so I had to do the same thing in another pharmacy. By this time the blood was running down my legs inside the pants I was wearing. The pills worked though. Three little pills but they really worked fast. Two weeks later I had the hysterectomy and the doctors apologized to me. He said he didn't realize how bad I was. I had endometriosis on all my organs.

CHAPTER 81

Besides all of this my first grandchild had been born eight weeks early and one month to the day after my surgery. He had to be in the hospital four and a half weeks and was not only an early baby he was sick with the same virus my daughter had which made her go into labor early. I stayed in the hospital with my daughter that first night even though the weasel and everyone else said I didn't need to. The weasel's cousin and his family were at our house for the weekend but I knew they would understand. It was the weasel who didn't. The baby's lung collapsed in the night and he had to have surgery. I was so glad I had stayed. The baby had so many tubes running in and out of him but when I put my finger in his hand he closed his little hand around it. I told his dad and other grandma but they said he didn't do that with them. He didn't even weigh 4 pounds but when that little hand squeezed my finger I called him my lifeline and knew we needed each other. I was so glad to be there that night to pray and I promised God that if he would save the baby I would make sure the baby knew who had saved him. My daughter had me to make phone calls but nobody came. I was so miserable with the weasel but when the baby came home she didn't want anyone but me to watch him. The weasel had lost his job and I had applied for two jobs and got them both. So I was working a full-time and part time job plus babysitting. I guess it was good that I could survive without much sleep.

CHAPTER 82

About four weeks before I started the two jobs though I was going back-and-forth about 70 miles between the two hospitals where my grandson and my brother were. My daughter was still sick and pumping milk to take care of the baby. One day at the hospital one of the nurses told me she heard everyone telling me I didn't need to stay. She said you were right! If that had been my daughter and grandbaby there is no way I would have left.

CHAPTER 83

My brother had put off his open-heart surgery until the middle of the week. I was able to be there but I had to wait my turn to see him. When I saw him it was the first time I had ever seen fear in his face. He had always been so strong. I knew instantly what was wrong and wondered why no one else could tell. It was so obvious. He still had the tube down his throat and that makes you feel like you can't breathe. There was sheer terror in his turquoise Paul Newman eyes. There was a nurse in the room but she was looking out the window with her back to us. I went and got her told her I was his sister and the tube was scaring him. She explained to him that in a little while, when he settled down they would remove it. After that I talked to my brother. I told him I could tell how scared he was but he had to calm down. He nodded his head and then I saw the terror leave his eyes. I had to leave then to get over my own fear. I knew I couldn't cry in front of him. But when I went to the waiting room after I had composed myself. I asked everyone why they couldn't tell what was wrong.

CHAPTER 84

For years my brother would ask me if things were OK. I couldn't tell him the weasel was treating me so bad. He would have stopped it but with his bad heart it could have been the end of him. I had been praying for him for so many years but he hadn't accepted Jesus as his Savior yet. He did that at 69 years old though and lived to be 79.

CHAPTER 85

Now back to when I was working so hard and homeless after the divorce. My brother and his second wife had a very small house. I would go there after work to take a shower. I couldn't stay at Rachel's house because she and her husband weren't getting along and my ex stayed at Rebecca's just so I couldn't. He had our house but wouldn't stay there. So I had no choice but to sleep on sister's couch part time or in an old house that belonged to my aunt with no heat. That was my two choices, listen to my mom, who had gradually taken over my younger sister's life or be cold sleeping in a lawn chair chaise. I tried to wait as long as I could stopping somewhere to get a sandwich but no matter how late it was mom would be waiting to start right in on me. You can't flush the stool. Don't make any noise. I would just lie down on the couch with my back to her and pretend to sleep. While she rambled on. I finally decided it was better to be cold. So I just slept in the old house. I kept hearing something I thought was mice but one night I found a mama possum and her babies coming in from a hole in the floor.

CHAPTER 86

During these long months I did any kind of work I could get with my clothes and tools in an old car with a rod knocking. I worked long hours double shifts at the minimart painted for two apartment complexes and cleaned, painted and wallpapered for lots of old people who trusted me because I was a woman. I never had to advertise because I was so good at what I did especially painting. I started out at five dollars an hour but kept getting faster through the years and gradually increase to 12.50 an hour.

CHAPTER 87

By now I had learned not to trust anyone so I saved every penny I could and carried it in my jean's pockets, the bills anyway. I had dreaded to go to sister's house but I didn't mind the cold house. When we were kids my older sister and I slept in the room that was the farthest from the coal stove catty corner. It was so cold that when I took a glass of water in there at night to wet my hair to pin curl it the little bits of water in the glass the next morning was frozen.

CHAPTER 88

After a few months the rod in my car was knocking louder so I went to a junkyard and asked if they had a car that would run. They did but I didn't have quite enough money. I was blessed with friends I had gotten to know by working for them. One wonderful woman offered to cosign for me at the bank to get the junkyard car. She was a very influential woman so the bank didn't even hesitate. I was amazed that she thought that much of me when she hadn't known me very long. So I traded in the car with the rod knocking for a little car that lasted me several years. I thank God that he was blessing me even though I had gotten a divorce.

One night when I was working at the minimart the town cop from Gravelton came up to talk to me. He said do you have a gun and can you shoot one? I told him I could shoot but my ex-husband got all his guns and my two guns. All I got was my holster and the only reason I got it was because it wouldn't fit my ex. The cop then said well you better borrow a gun because your ex is driving past that old house you're staying in all night every night. He said he was trying to watch out for me but he also had to patrol the other end of town. Later when the divorce was final my ex asked if I ever loved him. I told him yes. Then he said, "oh! And I suppose I killed that love." I said, "you said it yes you did." Then he told me he would spend the rest of his life getting even with me for leaving him. I think he is even with me if he would count all the lies, the affairs, the years of abuse. Doing most of his work because he was so lazy. A chiropractor told me I have shaken adult syndrome in my neck and if it had been a baby I would be dead. He never shook my babies though but he did spank them so hard once he left his red handprints on their butts. They were four and six and I didn't say it in front of them but after I got them to bed I told him if he ever left marks on them again he would be sorry. He knew me well enough that he knew it wasn't an idle threat and I think if I hadn't threatened him he would have beat them too like his dad did. His mom told me that he beat them especially the oldest boy.

When he got drunk he would get his shotgun and make them all get out of the house. Then when he passed out they would go back in. He cussed them calling them bitches and bastards. The kids hated him except the one I married. He said it was OK for him to cuss as long as they didn't cuss him back. The one I married was just like his dad but he didn't whip them again. I would have killed him and he knew it. But he did abuse me. Shook me, choked me and then threatened to kill me. His dad was nice sober and mean drunk. My ex was the opposite. Nice drunk but mean as hell sober.

After the town cop warned me about my ex I borrowed a shotgun. But it was getting cold in that big old house with no heat. I had an old electric blanket but the plug-ins were so worn out they wouldn't hold the plug I had some money saved so I started driving around in the other small town looking for a place to live. I know this shouldn't go right here but I just thought of it and don't want to forget. I was working in the minimart one night before the divorce was final when the weasel came in and said, "are you ever coming back because I'm not gonna live without sex. So if you're not coming back I'm gonna fix the house up and get me another woman." I said, "you sure weren't helping me fix it up. You just laid on your lard butt and let me do the work that's been done on it. But you're going to work on it to get a woman for sex? No I will never come back. I shouldn't have stayed with you as long as I did and I could never stand for you to touch me again."

I almost killed him once by accident. He worked the midnight shift and I heard something so I grabbed the 357 magnum that he told me to keep under my pillow. I had never shot it but he said just pull the top back on it to cock it if I ever needed it. I went into the family room with my left hand on top of it but didn't cock it. As he came in the other end of the room he turned white and started shaking. He said, "don't you ever point that GD gun at me." I said, "I didn't cock it and I didn't know it was you." But he just kept saying that over and over and I kept saying I didn't know it was you when I heard a noise. He sat up the rest of the night smoking cigarettes. I asked him if he was coming to bed. He said, "leave me alone. Go to bed." A few years later my son-in-law said, "I want to ask you something. Why did you sleep with that gun under your pillow?" I said. "it wasn't cocked." He said. "I beg your pardon. I used to go in there and look at it and it was always cocked. There was always a shell in the chamber and I have shot it and it had a hair trigger. If you had bumped it, it would have blown your head off." I started shaking probably about how the weasel shook when he knew the gun was cocked and I didn't. He was hoping I would be killed. The sad thing was I used to lay our first grandson on that bed for naps. That was just another reason that proved to me the weasel didn't care about anyone but himself.

All those years I never told anyone how he treated me and how afraid I was. Not even my daughter had any idea. He was so two-faced no one even suspected. My daughters would get off the bus and I would be fixing supper. They always noticed my face being red from crying. One of them always said, "what's wrong mom?" And I always said. "oh! You know how easy I cry." When they learned the truth Rachel said she was glad she didn't know in school. She is the bashful one like I used to be. No one knew the truth for years but it was like with mom I was too afraid to tell anyone. Just think though for 50 years I lived with all kinds of abuse. People don't always look like what they're going through.

We lived in that house six months before I left with no water heater. I had to heat water in pans on the stove to take a bath. That didn't bother the lazy weasel. He just didn't take baths. Six months without a bath. Back to my searching for a place to live. Eventually I found an old house that you could barely see for the weeds. I found out that a couple had just moved out and left it 30 some years before. It looked like they had left in a hurry. Little bit of a mystery. When I found them they said when they moved back to the area but they were too old to fix it up so just bought another house.

When the old man and his brother-in-law came to show it to me he didn't even have a key. We had to take a piece of paneling off of a broken window and crawl in. I was wondering if my friend might cosign for me again since I had the car paid in full. The house was in terrible shape and the neighbors thought it would have to be torn down. But I could see the potential in it since I had fixed up so many old houses. I asked the old man if he would sell it to me. When he said yes and told me the price I almost fell. I had enough money. So I took a $100 bill out of my pocket and gave it to him for a down payment. Then I found an old scrap of paper and ask him to write me a receipt. When I met his wife and she heard the price he had quoted me she said he should have given it to you. It took a while to get the abstract brought up to date and I was working hard long hours to make enough money to start fixing up the house. Eventually it was mine.

I thanked God again but wondered how he could be blessing me when I had gotten a divorce. God hates divorce. A man whom I didn't know at all had started helping me and that had brought more threats from my ex. One day, while I was working my sis let the man in the old house where I was staying to put in a new receptacle so I could plug in that old electric blanket. My ex called me and said you're going to cause me to kill someone. I saw that long-legged bastard at the house where you're staying. I assumed he had seen the man's vehicle so I said am I there? Remember you're calling me at work. This man even tried to talk to my ex. He told me he had met him at a park but when my ex started to talk bad about me he said he told him, "hey I didn't come here to hear this. She needs help and I'm going to help her. If I saw a dog along the road needing help I would help the dog." Now by this time I was so scared I had to be hospitalized. Even though I was calling him my ex the actual court day hadn't come yet. I had a nervous breakdown. The doctor had left strict orders to keep me sedated. All I knew was my soon to be ex kept calling me to threaten me and told me he had canceled my hospitalization insurance which was illegal since the divorce wasn't final. But in my mind it was final the day I stood outside the house and told him to shoot me. I knew at that time I would rather be dead than ever have him touch me again.

There is something else I haven't told about yet. Before we moved into town my ex insisted that we get a satellite dish when we couldn't afford it. Then when the kids weren't home he would watch pornography. This is the hardest part to talk about. He became obsessed with anal sex and tried to force me to do it. I told him this is my body and I have a right to say what happens to it. Of course he told me again that he owned me and he was the man and that I should do whatever he told me. I told him you can own a dog. Not a person. The last time he almost got it done because he had put Vaseline on himself. Then he grabbed me around the waist and it was hard to get away. He sure knew where to put the bruises where they didn't show. But I did get away from him and then I told him you almost got it done that time but if you had of I would feel so dirty and degraded I would've killed myself but I would have killed you first. He knew I meant it and since I didn't obey him things got so bad I knew I couldn't stay much longer. I tried to reason with him. I told him we had two houses and to take the one he wanted and let me have the other. Reasoning wouldn't work with him. When we finally went to court he brought my youngest daughter with him. He knew I wouldn't talk about it in front of her. So here I am. I know I'm much smarter than him but a person like him who only thinks about ways to control other people can do it because they never feel guilty. The only thing is they don't think they will ever be punished for the wrongs they have done. You can't hide evil from God. He sees and hears every evil deed they think they have hidden. It will all be revealed when they think they have gotten away with it.

If I don't stop I don't think I will get this book finished. I hope it can help people with similar tortures in their lives. Remember there are givers and there are takers. There are abusers and there are victims.

CHAPTER 89

During my senior year of school in Gravelton I stayed with my aunt and crazy uncle. I could have stayed with grandma, daddy's mom, but mom wanted me to stay with her brother. Mom wouldn't come to my graduation and I sang with two classmates at our baccalaureate. We sang *Ivory Palaces*. But since mom wouldn't come daddy didn't either. He knew she would make his life miserable if he did something to show he cared about me. Mom always told me my younger sister was daddy's favorite but she just said it to hurt me. My older siblings and I knew better. When daddy passed, mom wouldn't go to the funeral home or to the dinner after the funeral. My younger sister wouldn't go in the casket room. My older siblings told me to pick out everything because they knew I was his favorite and they both said they wanted me to be satisfied. Of course mom gripped about everything and after I stood by the casket the whole four hours the funeral home people forgot who I was and seated me at the back. When I mentioned it later mom said I should have come up front and sat at her feet. That's where she always wanted me anyway at her feet to trample on.

CHAPTER 90

We seniors got out of school a few days early and my aunt was a teacher so she wasn't home. My friend took me to my parent's house a few days later. But in the meantime my crazy drunk uncle started telling me that lots of women kept leaving notes in his mailbox telling him anytime. He said he could have any one he wanted. The problem was he wanted me. He came over to me rubbed my leg and asked me to kiss him. I just shook my head no. His face got really red. I thought he was going to rape me. But he said get your stuff I'm taking you to Zelphia's. After he dropped me off Zelphia called mom and she came right down. She told us she would take care of it. She was gone for a long time and when she came back Zelphia asked her what happened. She said she took care of it and she didn't want to hear anymore about it ever.

CHAPTER 91

A FEW YEARS LATER MOM LEFT my younger sister with them to go to school so I knew then for sure that he had lied out of it and mom had believed him instead of me. They probably had a glass of wine together. I had seen them argue before with both their faces beet red. I had seen him screaming at my aunt. She didn't say a word. She was so scared of him. Mom and her brother were mentally unbalanced. That combined with drinking wine and it's sure to be trouble.

CHAPTER 92

Back now to the day of the divorce Don had asked me to go out to eat. On the way I remembered that I hadn't told sis where I was going. This was before cell phones so we stopped at a big grocery store. The end of the store was all big windows. The phone was on the wall right at the end of the windows. There was no one around so I was crying and talking. I said the judge didn't give me one of our houses but at least I wouldn't have to worry about my ex trying to force me to have anal sex. When I turned to leave there was a man in a wheelchair. As I walked past him he said, "I'm sorry." I told him I was the one that should feel sorry for him. He said, "No. I heard you talking. You have every right to cry." As I looked at him I couldn't help noticing his eyes. They were piercing and a shade of blue I had never seen before. I thanked him and went to Don's vehicle just outside the windows. I looked back into the store assuming the man in the wheelchair would be using the phone. I asked Don if he had seen the man. He said, "No. I looked all around but there was no one there." I knew then that I had talk to an angel. I had heard of people talking to angels but I never thought it would happen to me. I even asked the people in the store if they knew the man. No one did.

CHAPTER 93

I HAD BEEN PRAYING EVERY NIGHT before bed begging God to not give up on me. I knew God hated divorce and I thought he wouldn't want me anymore. That was the devil deceiving me. I know now that even though God hates divorce it's not unforgivable.

CHAPTER 94

Sometime later Don asked me to marry him but I told him I couldn't because I didn't believe in divorce so how could I remarry? I stayed single for five years then I talked to five different preachers. After they heard about my past life they all said they thought I was free to remarry. I told them the hardest part was forgiving myself. But one of the preachers wives said if I didn't forgive myself it was like I was putting myself above God because God had forgiven me When I kept begging for forgiveness. Five years later we did get married. I knew he loved me and later we were both re-baptized. The most amazing thing I have finally learned is that God not only forgives but he forgets. That is so awesome but we do serve an awesome God.

CHAPTER 95

Don helped me fix up the old house I bought. I also hired a man who did a lot of the work. While I was still working on the house I tried to get insurance on it but the agent said two big trees had to be removed before they would insure it. The man I hired to take out the trees just stared at me for a long time. Finally he said you are a survivor. He didn't realize what he said and I didn't either until we both stood there staring at each other. Finally I said I guess I am. Even now I wonder how I stayed alive. I guess God wasn't done with me.

CHAPTER 96

We lived in that house 13 years. Then when a house became available here in Gravelton we moved here. I sold the other house on contract for two years supposedly then they were supposed to get a loan. But this was a big mistake. Trusting them. They let their daughter move in with her two kids. I didn't go in to check the house often enough because I was working on this house and they mailed the payments. After two years they couldn't get the loan and I had to force them to leave. I had to go in to get a door that belonged to my dad. That was when I realized they had completely trashed the house. When I was standing at the top of the stairs the man got real smart with me so I had to take a police officer with me when I went back. I asked the man if he wanted to smart off to me in front of the officer and my husband. Of course he didn't but the house was so bad I couldn't stand to fix it up again. None of them were young children but they had written on the walls, put out cigarettes on the floor, among other gross things so I filed bankruptcy on it. The house I'm in now also needed so much I doubt if I'll ever get it done but I've done enough most of it is livable.

CHAPTER 97

Don is a Christian. We both love God. That means so much to me and I'm sure he will never touch me in a mean way like the weasel. He loves me and even wrote a beautiful song about me.

CHAPTER 98

This is another story about my health. I had a lot of problems with my digestive system. Some of my friends used to come watch me drink my prune juice. I had several colonoscopies. The one I had in 1987 was probably the fourth. That one took almost 3 times as long as they had told me. I watched the clock as the doctor and his two assistants had to take turns working on me. Then one year later the Doctor who did the hysterectomy said he had to straighten my colon because it was in knots.

CHAPTER 99

Then in 1998 I had another colonoscopy. The doctor that did that one had the best reputation in the area and when he talked to me in his office the next week he asked me about my life and told me my colon needed to be removed. He said it was so kinked and rigid it would never work. Also he said colons like mine was always found in abused women. I knew I didn't want to live that way so for two more years I suffered with it. I used every kind of prescription and over-the-counter meds. I even tried coffee enemas. Nothing really worked. Then one day I was in the bathroom listening to a preacher on the television in the bedroom. I still don't know who the preacher was but he said something I had never heard before. He said you don't have to keep begging for your healing it's already yours. He said according to 1st Peter 2:24 which says by his stripes you were healed. That the word were is past tense so healing belongs to you. Then he said just claim it in Jesus' name and start thanking him for it. I was so tired of trying every way I knew how to get my colon to work I was desperate. So I called Don who was away working and said I wasn't going to struggle with it anymore. My stomach swelled up but I really believed I was healed. Three days later my colon started working. That was in 2000, 17 years ago, and it still works. The people from the doctor's office kept calling and sending letters for me to come back for another colonoscopy. I kept telling them I was healed but they were skeptical.

CHAPTER 100

Then in 2013 my cat bit me playing around. By morning the infection was all the way up my arm so my doctor sent me to the hospital. The bite had turned to cellulitis. When the bloodwork was analyzed they said I was anemic and would have to have tests including a colonoscopy. The same doctor did the test that had done them in 1998. The girls in his office had told me he remembered everyone. So when they took me in for the colonoscopy I asked him if he remembered me. He said yes. Then when he was finished and I woke up he came up to see me. Patted my arm and said, "honey your colon is perfect." I told him I knew it was because when God heals something it's healed. I think this happened to increase his faith and the others in the room who were helping him. It is really true though. God works in mysterious ways.

CHAPTER 101

Now back to when I was young. I had lots of friends. One would come to our house, get down on her knees, and beg mom to let me go to the little café in town. Sometimes after Dory had begged for almost an hour mom would let me go around 7:30. But I had to be back in the house by 9 PM. Once in a while when we were dancing and having so much fun I would forget to watch the clock. So she would send daddy to get me. When we were walking home I would ask daddy why does mom have to be like she is? Why can't I do things like the other kids? Daddy always gave me the same answer, "I don't know but we just have to try to get along with her." We both knew that was impossible. She was always mad and screaming at one of us for who knows what.

CHAPTER 102

One of my friends used to ask me to come to her house to study. Her parents were always good to me. But mom hated me so bad she just couldn't stand for me to think anyone liked me. So when I would get back from their house she would start in on me. Saying they don't really like you. They just want to keep their little Hellenie at home.

CHAPTER 103

Back to the neurologist who named what I had one time when we were talking, she had said I had PTSD. I told her I thought that was just soldiers. She said no it was anyone who was afraid of losing their lives.

CHAPTER 104

Two kinds of people share the world. Which ones will make it through?
There's givers and there's takers. My friend which kind are you?

The givers keep on giving and they always give their best.
The takers take all they can get and then ask where is the rest?

The givers give their heart and soul to anyone in need.
The takers laugh and mock them because that's the takers creed.

The givers give all they can give and asked nothing in return.
They try to teach their takers love but the takers never learn.

The givers have the warmest hearts. The takers heart's like ice
the givers give love freely but to get love pay the price.

In some ways the takers give. It all depends on gain.
While they take all the credit they give givers all of the blame.

The takers take all givers give but they will give advice.
The givers give the takers all and get the worst from life.

But in the end when their life is gone the truth will then unfold.
While the takers walk on hot coals the givers streets of gold.

CHAPTER 105

I THINK SOME OF MY WRITINGS and poems might show people how I got through the hard times.

Love dies.

When no one's there to hold you love dies.
When no one understand you love dies.

When you wait for years for some day to feel loved that special way. But you never see that day, love dies.
You wake one day to realize;

the love you knew is gone.
You look into the same eyes, you've been looking in so long.

You try again to find the look you know is just not there.
And just ignore that old look that says he doesn't care.

For years, you've tried to make right. What's always been so wrong.
How can you make it right today? You've already tried too long.

You can't really remember; how long ago it's been,
but somewhere between right and wrong, your love came to an end!

CHAPTER 106

I DON'T KNOW IF SOME OF my songs and poems will help anyone. But they helped me get through some rough tough times. My ex used to say bad things about some of my friends and relatives but when he said my cousin's little boy got killed because of something my cousin did when he was a teenager I had to remind him that he wasn't God.

CHAPTER 107

Another story about mom. She would soak her feet in a foot tub every night. When the water got cool enough she would let little sis sit in her little rocking chair and put her feet in. I was about nine or 10 and I asked every night if I could put my feet in. One night she finally said yes but as soon as I put my feet in and my foot touched mom's she said, "see I told you there wasn't room." So I took my feet back out and never asked again.

CHAPTER 108

Back when I was a teenager some evenings when Dory and her parents were at our house and my mom wouldn't let me go to the little restaurant in town where we danced Dory and I would just sit at the table with our parents. But Mom would just keep blowing smoke in my face. I would ask her to stop but she wouldn't and said she did it to make sure I wouldn't smoke. I would promise her that I never would but she would just keep doing it so I would go in the other room. And sometimes Dory and her mom would be singing and I like hearing them. Mom just wanted to be mean to me any way she could.

CHAPTER 109

ONE TIME THE EX DECIDED we should have a restaurant in town. He promised that he would learn to cook on the grill so I could have some time off. But, of course, he didn't. We opened at 5 AM and closed at 11 PM and all the weasel did was make coffee then sat and drink it with the customers. The girls were raised but the youngest still lived at home and helped sometimes. She babysat for her cousin some too but once she was there with the two of her classmates and I had told her not to be there if her cousin had any men there. We found out she and her friends were there so the weasel and I went to get her. When we stopped one of the two men opened the door then tried to close it. Of course the cowardly weasel didn't even get out of the truck. I pushed the door open with such force the man almost fell and told him to get out of my way. Then I told my daughter to get in her car and get home. Two or three nights later my daughter's cousin came in our restaurant. I was in the kitchen. She came back there and told me Rebecca was 18 and I couldn't legally make her leave any place. I said we had an agreement that if any men were there Rebecca could not be. Then I said she still lives at home and she broke our agreement. And I would come after her if it happened again. Then when we got home my ex slapped her in the face so I got between them.

Once Rebecca was asked to sing with a boy she had graduated with at a wedding about 1 1/2 blocks from the restaurant but the weasel threw a fit so I didn't get to hear them. That was the only time that she sang somewhere that I didn't get to hear her. Nothing I wanted to do ever mattered to the weasel and I was always too afraid of him to defy him. He could've watched the restaurant for an hour but he wouldn't.

CHAPTER 110

Back to when we ran the service station. When daddy found out they tried to hire me aside from the station and they had said I outsmarted the computer he was so proud of me. But he made mom mad again when he bragged about me. She said he's told everyone he knows. Then when we would visit them she was so jealous when he talked to me she would tell him to go in another room. He would then I would go there to talk to him. When I went back I really got the evil eye.

Oh! And talk about intuition. My first daughter wouldn't let mom hold her but she would let daddy hold her. My other daughter one time when she was nine and I came in crying said, "I am going to tell grandma to stop making you cry." I wouldn't let her but when my brother heard about it he said I should have let her.

CHAPTER 111

There are so many stories I could tell but here's another one. I had some birthday money from some relative. I had seen a skirt in a store window that I really liked. It was stripes around of all colors. I thought it would match every blouse I had. But mom knew I really liked it so she said I couldn't buy it. I said mom it's my birthday money. So after lots of arguing she finally let me buy it. But she had an ulterior motive. Always! Because that's the way her mind worked. I only had I think four skirts so I wore it a lot. She said every time I wore it people would say, "here she comes in that same skirt" when actually she was the only one who said it. Other people thought it was beautiful. Then one day when no one else was home but her and me she came in the room where I was with that skirt on. She said. "see I'm not that much bigger than you." Nobody cared. I could see that the button was about ready to rip off so I said, "please mom take it off before you ruin it." She wouldn't and she started dancing around in it while I kept begging her to stop. Finally I stopped begging which I knew was what she wanted. So she went in the bedroom and took it off. There was never another word said about what she did but I wished I had someone to talk to about it. Daddy just thought we had to try to get along with her. There was no way. After she poisoned or nagged daddy to death she continued to torture me until she died. Getting even! That's how she and my ex thought.

CHAPTER 112

I REMEMBER THE WEASEL WAS MAD at someone one time and he said he was going to put dog shit in his car seat. Also he said I'll see him out on the road sometime in the winter with his car broke down and I'll just give him the finger and go on by. He grated his teeth as he said it.

CHAPTER 113

Here's another story. My crazy uncle had been asked to be a pallbearer at someone's funeral. No one had much back then. So he had to borrow a suit. When he put it on the pants were too short. Mom's sister kind of laughed and teased him but he got mad and said he would get even with her. I guess there are lots of people like them. Then there are the rest of us that are the victims who can't forget.

CHAPTER 114

I WISH I COULD START AN organization for victims who don't think they have anyone to talk to. If a child is abused instead of taking the child out of the environment take the abuser out and lock them up. Take my word for it. People do not change and most kids don't lie if they get the nerve to speak up. Mom is gone but the ex is still here to plot another way to get even by using my daughters. I had pasted wallpaper for my aunt and picked strawberries but my first real job was in Hammond.

CHAPTER 115

I TOOK A JOB AS A carhop for two Greek women. I was getting ready for my first night's work when daddy asked me how much they were going to pay me? I said I didn't know so he said he would take me. He said I was to ask how much my salary was going to be. He backed his car in across from the window where I was to turn in the orders. This was in 1958. When I asked them what daddy said to ask they said I was supposed to turn in my Tips in a cup right inside the window and they would pay me $12 a week. When I told them that was my dad in his car and went to tell daddy he said to tell them I couldn't work for that but I would finish the week. Daddy would park there each night and take me home at 10 before he had to go to his job at 11. He told me to bring him part of my tips when I wasn't busy which he kept for me. He was trying to teach me how to make it in this world.

CHAPTER 116

THE NEXT JOB I GOT was also a car hop but I asked before I took the job. Now I know why they wanted my tips. I made around $75 a week in April on the dayshift. The girls who had worked there the year before said they averaged $100 a week when the weather was warmer.

CHAPTER 117

Now one more story about when we were juniors in high school. My friend the one who my brother gave his new shirt to was a great musician had asked a friend and I to sing with him at the sports banquet. We were really nervous but it got worse when he told us what we were going to sing. It was a popular song but in the chorus we had to sing Eya! Eya! Eya! I think The name of it was *Hula Love*. I said come on but we did it. And got a lot of applause. My friend played his guitar. I am including some more of my songs because writing them helped me get through the bad times. I sincerely hope they can help other people. I pray they will.

CHAPTER 118

Sometime during Danny's senior year a recruiter came to the school. Danny and some friends signed up for the Marines. Danny was only 17 but mom signed the paper for him to go after school was out. I said, "mom what if he changes his mind? By you signing he can't change his mind." I was so mad at her. Danny accepted it and told me he had to go get toughened up. He wanted me to punch him in the stomach. Then he would say is that all the harder you can hit? He was just a skinny kid who vomited a lot.

CHAPTER 119

HE TOLD ME A STORY about an officer that did something he didn't like so Danny wouldn't salute him. Then the wimp went and told the commanding officer on Danny. Then he was told he had to salute him. So Danny said, "but I don't respect him." So the higher officer said, "then you have to salute the uniform." So Danny said when he saw the man he would snap to attention and say, "to the uniform sir." But that wimp should not have been allowed to wear the uniform of a United States Marine after he had two of his buddies hold Danny while he beat him in the stomach. Danny didn't tell. He took it like a man.

CHAPTER 120

Another about my ex. When he decided to move to Gravelton it had to be right now even though my daughters were scheduled to dance in their dance class recital in a few days. Had their outfits and everything. I know they were young but it meant a lot to them and to me. The weasel thought everyone should obey him because he was the man. But I know now he was just a weasel in disguise. He wouldn't take them back for the recital and wouldn't let me. I'm so ashamed I didn't have the nerve to stand up to him.

A Weasel in Disguise

I used to think I hated men but I didn't understand,
there's men and then there's weasels that take the form of man.

If you don't know if you have one here's the telltale signs.
I know because for years I had a weasel to call mine.

They spit and scratch. They smoke and drink. Tell dirty jokes and lie.
They put you down, laugh at your friends, and mock you when you cry.

They tell you they're a better man than anyone you know.
That others are much sneakier, they just don't let it show.

Chorus; so watch closely when you meet a man, for his beady little eyes.
He might not be a man at all, just a weasel in disguise.

Rhoda Lane

They love themselves so much, there's no love left for you,
but they keep you to do things they can't, or just don't want to do.

They tease you about your body, though there's had gone to pot.
I guess when they look in the mirror, they see sir Lancelot.

If you don't have a real man, you're better off alone.
Because you don't have much, if all you have is a weasel of your own.

CHAPTER 121

Every time I think I'm done with this book I think of another story that should be included. One time when my parents were visiting and I had been wallpapering upstairs the baby went to sleep so I thought I could finish. I was trying to finish down the stairway when daddy came in and tried to help me by holding the bottom of a strip. Then mom came in and said, "well he never helped me." She started yelling. I was trying to calm her down when she said. "don't you think I would like to hang wallpaper?" Not much of anything she said ever made sense.

CHAPTER 122

One other time after one of his heart attacks he hadn't been eating much. He happened to stop by on one of his walks. I was putting supper on the table. Fried chicken, mashed potatoes, and all other things that go with it. Daddy sat down and ate with us. Now you would think mom might be glad but she said, "well if he likes your cooking better than mine he can just eat at your house from now on." Really crazy right?

CHAPTER 123

Needing a new furnace makes me think of another one. We needed one years ago and my ex told the man, I want the biggest one you got. The man said the biggest one will heat a warehouse. And if you put it in your house it would just run more and cost more. We didn't need it but my stupid ex said, "I don't care. I want the biggest one you got." I lived with a lot of dumb people for most of my life.

CHAPTER 124

But after we moved back and got settled in and made some friends it could have been OK. If the weasel would have treated me better. The friends we made were fun. The man and the weasel both played guitar. And we would sing. Their kids and ours were close to the same ages and got along really well.

CHAPTER 125

The weasel was so two-faced when we weren't with them he would call them names and make fun of them. It made me feel like our friendship with them was not real.

CHAPTER 126

Our friends went to the same church grandma had so my girls and I talked my ex in to going. After we had gone for a while I went forward to accept Jesus as my savior. I was 33. My girls were ages eight and 10 and they followed me. Then their dad followed. He tried for a while to act like he had changed but soon went back to his old self. He wouldn't stop making fun of our friends and calling them names. When I had the surgery so I could have babies, I thought it would help our relationship. But it just made it worse. He just had something else to hold over me by saying he had a good job and would get them. If not he would quit his job and lay in jail.

CHAPTER 127

Now back to when I was 16. School had been going on for eight weeks and when my brother and I went to Gravelton for the weekend. I had officially quit school. Because I was too nervous to change to a big school. Mom had said, "you don't need to graduate anyway you'll just get married." She hadn't graduated so she didn't want me to. Well when we were in Gravelton my friends talked me into staying. We didn't have a phone so I called the people in the downstairs apartment and had them to get daddy on the phone. He wanted me to graduate so I knew he would say yes. I don't know why I even wanted to stay. But I did. Daddy never told me about the hell he went through from mom for letting me stay. I knew it happened. It always happened. That's probably what caused his next heart attack. My decision to stay was unfair to daddy and my brother. I had been taking Danny to work because he had lost his license. So he had to drive back with no license. Bill was waiting for me to come back. I didn't know what I was doing. Back to daddy though, I don't know what that doctor meant years later when she said your mom probably killed your dad. Even if she didn't poison him she probably nagged him to death. I was so unfair to Daddy, Danny and Bill. My decisions started the trail to my ruining my Life. It was my own fault.

CHAPTER 128

I HAVE TO TELL THE STORY about my brother. You've heard the saying he'll give you the shirt off of his back. My brother actually did that. My friend's band was playing one year at our high school homecoming years ago. They used to have dances. My friend that I graduated with had his own band. This one year my brother had bought an expensive western shirt to wear. When he walked by my friend and my friend told him how pretty it was my brother just took it off and gave it to my friend. And he took my friends old black T-shirt. I've never known any other people like my dad and brother. They both just gave up their own hopes and dreams to accommodate the rest of us. I was so busy thinking and telling people how smart they both were I didn't know how I took advantage of them. I was just thinking about ways to get away from mom even for a little while. By getting away from her, by staying in Gravelton for school my future was ruined. My dad had it the worst though. My uncle, daddy's brother, told my cousin if her mom had of treated him like mom treated daddy he would have coldcocked her. That's an old fashion saying meaning knocked her out!

CHAPTER 129

My brother was going with a girl when he and her brother joined the Marines. She promised to wait for him. She was still in school and as far as we knew still planning to marry Danny. They wrote back-and-forth and he sent her gifts. All the time she was dating some rich man and didn't tell my brother until he came home. Danny was devastated and started drinking more all the time. I was so mad at her and I told Danny his drinking was her fault. He told me not to be mad at her. He said maybe someday I'll find a cute little girl with a big nose like you. He did but before that something else happened. Sounds like a soap opera doesn't it? But just wait!

CHAPTER 130

After I graduated I took a friend back to Hammond with me well actually she took me. She had worked and had her own car which was neat. What I noticed was she had white leather gloves. We both got a restaurant job and I was the car hop. I spilled a root beer on a customer. I'm glad it was a man. A woman might not have been so nice. But he was nice about it and still gave me a tip. Eventually my friend got pregnant with my brother's baby. Just another thing mom blamed on me and even though she said my friend could stay with us. Blame game! And I did feel bad about it but it could have worked out for them if three troublemakers from our hometown had not traveled all those miles to do what they like best, to cause trouble. Danny shouldn't have a listened to them and meant to just put off the wedding for a while. He had already bought the rings but it didn't work out.

CHAPTER 131

By this time I had already married my first husband. I knew it was a mistake right away but I just couldn't admit it. That would have meant mom was right. She hated my ex and he hated her. I figured out later it was because they were two of a kind. Control freaks! If I hadn't had my daughters those years would have just been a complete waste!

CHAPTER 132

My brother paid support for his son and planned to talk to him when he turned 18. But he was killed in an accident at 17. My brother was always sorry that he didn't marry my friend but to this day she calls me her sister-in-law. Things just didn't seem to work out for Danny or me. It was mostly messes of our own making.

CHAPTER 133

My brother did marry a girl with a big nose like me but that's where the similarities end. Danny didn't know her well enough. She ran around with other men and later bragged about it. The two kids she had are drug addicts. They've been in prison. The first is back in prison now and the second one doesn't even belong to my brother. He told me and he would know. They both stole from him and sold his stuff for their drugs. The first one doesn't look anything like Danny so who knows. The boy my friend had did look like my brother and my friend said he even had Danny's beautiful turquoise eyes.

CHAPTER 134

I TOLD MY GRANDDAUGHTER HOW MUCH I admire her. She just got a divorce with two kids. She is so much braver than I was. She now is going to college and holding down a job and still manages to have their supper ready in the crockpot which she starts before she leaves in the morning.

I cried my tears alone

He said he saw you in a bar. Crying in your beer.
She said she'd never seen a man, cry such big 'ol tears.

They didn't see the tears I cried. I cried my tears at home.
I didn't want the world to know, so I cried my tears alone.

I wonder when you're sitting there if you think how every day
your wife cried lots of tears like that, before she walked away?

Do you think as your drinking buddies gather around you there
you were the one who saw her tears and didn't even care

you have your friends to dry your tears mine dried on their own
I didn't want the world to know so I cried my tears alone.

Maybe if I'd been like you and gone out to a bar
the people who now dry your tears would see you as you are.

But you and I both know the truth we know who made us cry.
You never thought the tears that fall could be from your own eyes.

Born with a broken heart and then blamed for crying

Away

Childhood dreams to be a dancer, singer, movie star.
Of working for an airline to travel oh so far.

Away from all the pain and fear a child should never know
but in her heart she knows there's really no place she can go.

Away! Away in dreams a world of make-believe away to fantasy forget she's been deceived away from things in life she should not have to know and in her world of make-believe

she finds a way to go. The child grows up and thinks that she's forgot the childhood dreams
but too soon find the grown-up world is not the way it seemed.

She dances to the radio when no one's there to see
and knows her world of make-believe is something she still needs.

After many years one day her way of thinking change. When she met the Lord of hosts her meager life became.

A walk she really knew someday would surely take her home.
Away from pain and sorrow 'cause the Lord calls her his own.

Away! Away in dreams but now the dreams are real.
Away from fantasy 'cause now her future is sealed.

And even if there's pain in life contented she will stay.
Because God has promised by his grace he will still take her away. Away! Away! Away! Away!

CHAPTER 135

Here's another one:

I've No More to Give

I look in the mirror and think who are you?
And who I want to be whispers please let me through.

But do I have the strength to let me outside?
When I've learned so well my true feelings to hide.

I try not to think and wouldn't dare to dream
because my life is now just a part of your scheme.

Two questions cloud my mind am I really me?
Or am I just someone you want me to be?

you want me to say what you want to hear
and keep right on smiling while I'm living in fear.

We vowed before God till death do us part
but death might be welcomed by my broken heart.

How far can I go and not compromise me?
How far can I go before I cease to be?

Because I'm just surviving. I don't really live
to find what's left of me I've no more to give

Born with a broken heart and then blamed for crying

you've always told me it's part of God's plan.
I must do as you say because you're the man.

But God took the darkness and let there be light.
He gave me a mind to know wrong from right.

Though I'm just a woman I still have a soul.
Lord give me my strength before I'm too old.

How far can I go to find what's left of me?
I hope it's not too late please God let it be.

Because I'm just surviving. I don't really live.
To find what's left of me, I have no more to give.

CHAPTER 136

I JUST HAVE A LITTLE MORE. Hope someone likes them.

CHAPTER 137

Most of my stories in my book are sad, but this is a cute funny story. When I was fourteen, my friend and I picked strawberries to make money at a local fruit farm.

Then her mom took us to a G. C. Murphy store where we each bought a linen suit with a straight skirt and jacket.

That fall I went to another city with my and aunt and uncle to visit another aunt and uncle. This was the aunt who always brought me my cousin's clothes. They were about the only clothes I had.

When we got there, they asked if we wanted to go to a movie. I wore my new brown suit with little flecks of yellow and white. My little cousin wore his Cub Scout uniform. When we got ready to go, my uncle went to my older cousin's closet and got her Mouton Jacket out for me to wear.

They took us to a real fancy theatre, told us to stay together and they would come back and get us.

My little cousin was the perfect little gentleman. He even escorted me upstairs to the bathroom. We really go a lot of stares from everyone. Everyone in the theatre couldn't quit looking at us. I was lots of fun.

Memories of Life

I wish I could sort through my memories. Just keep the good close to my heart.
Throw out all the sad along with the bad. The ones that still make teardrop start.

Rhoda Lane

I used to think we had some good times way back when I thought you loved me.
But good times fade fast into the past when shadowed by bad memories.

I kept thinking things will get better it's hard to admit when you're wrong.
Your love wasn't right and try as I might I couldn't stay I'm not that strong

Someday the bad memories will be gone when I can forget about you
somehow I'll erase the look on your face the look no one else ever knew.

The good memories of our children are so vivid now in my mind.
They come first with me and they'll always be the ones that are easy to find.

When I close my eyes I still see them.
I smile in my sweet dreams
but then the memories of you start slipping through
and I open my eyes once again.

If someone could invent a Camera to take movies of memories
then I could pray for amnesia. Someday to find a new person in me

then someone could cut out the bad things and I'd watch the rest till I knew
all the good things that life can bring but I'd never know I knew you.

Memories of life that are kept deep within.
Bad memories of things that shouldn't have been.

But they're fading now 'cause I'm starting to see how to replace the bad with the good memories that's all folks! Rhoda

-not quite all

Born with a broken heart and then blamed for crying

The Love In God's Grace

Sometimes when I'm trying, to perceive God's love, I try to imagine, that day up above, when it was decided, that Jesus should go, and live as a human, in this world below. You'll have to leave splendor, to live with the poor. You'll walk rocky roads, and sleep on the earth's floor. You know they'll reject you, and most won't believe. But maybe some would, if a virgin conceived.

When they see you heal blind eyes, cause lame legs to walk, and cast out a demon, so a mute man can talk. When they see you feed thousands, with a few loaves of bread,
and with only three words, give life to the dead.

When you say he without sin, should cast the first stone, and everyone leaves. The accused stands alone. Wont all of these things, make everyone see?

And say he's the Messiah. He's here to save me! That's what you would think, but some who were there, just couldn't untangle, the evil ones snare. They mocked him. They cursed him.
They crowned him with thorns. But Jesus knew this would happen, before he was born. This kind of love, humans can't understand.
This humiliation, our Lord endured as man.

He bore all our sins, as he carried the cross,
so don't turn away, and be one of the lost.

He said father forgive them. They know not what they do.
He bled, and he died, to save me, to save you.

So don't ever think, this can't happen for me.
The worst of the sinners, by his death can be freed.

And even the people, who spat in his face,
could have been forgiven, by the love in God's grace.

Rhoda Lane

For Heaven's Sake

You're busy working overtime, to pay for that new home.
You hardly see your wife and kids. They're at home alone.

You've got the boat, and two new cars, the cabin on the lake.
But what in the world are you doing, for heaven sake?

The weekends here. You take the time, to go out with your friends.
You drink a lot, and leave the bar, with an old girlfriend.

You think that you have all you need. You push God from your mind. You think, someday I'll go to church, when I have more time.

Chorus: but, what are you doing for heaven's sake? God's trying to warn you, of the chances you take. But, if you're not listening, God's heart you will break. Tell me, what are you doing, for heaven's sake?

You wake him Sunday afternoon, and start to question him. He says I give you everything, don't ask me where I've been. You cry alone, and think of how, he loved you in your youth. You think he's found another, but you just can't face the truth. You used to take the kids to church, now no one wants to go. Your family's headed different ways, and soon the world will know, your kids find comfort, with their friends, that they can't find at home. But mom can't see the danger. She has troubles of her own.

Chorus:

Your family's grown. You're growing old, but still don't have a plan.
You say, I bother no one. I just do the best I can.

You think you'll go to heaven, for the good life that you've led.
But if you've read God's book, you could see, that's not what Jesus said.

Chorus:
Tell me, what in the world are you doing?
What in the world are you doing?
What in the world are you doing, for heaven sake?

Born with a broken heart and then blamed for crying

It Takes Tears to Learn

A four-year-old, once said to me, do you know everything?
I told him, no only God knows what each day will bring.
But I do I know a lot of things, that it takes tears to learn,
like someone's love is not a thing, that you can ever earn.

Chorus:
Teardrop start, when broken hearts, finally face the truth.
Now I know, love can't grow, in someone like you.
For years I thought that things I did, could earn a person's love.
But for some people, everything would never be enough.
Those people don't know how to love.

The word means something else.
This took too many tears to learn, but teardrops teach so well.

Chorus:
Like fields of flower, love must have, a warm place it can grow.
But never try to plant love seeds, in a heart that's hard and cold.

I told him, there's some things I wish, I never had to know.
Too bad there's not a good way, to let bad memories go.

  This is a really good place to stop. It's not the end until God calls me home. This earth is not my home. It's just a place for my earthly body. When God calls me my Spirit will get a new body that will live forever with no more pain. God will wipe away my tears and make me forget all the bad things on this earth. The reason I have written my story is to encourage other people who are going through a similar life and tell them if I made it you can too! Just get close to Jesus. I know I couldn't have made it without him. Thank you heavenly father. Thank you Jesus my Savior. Thank you Holy Spirit. You are always with me. Jesus said, he would send you to be our comforter and he did.

  Just a little more during the late 70s and early 80s my ex cleared around $320-3 weeks and $260 the fourth week if he worked every night. He usually missed two or three nights a month. He expected me to manage the money. We had a house payment, a new truck payment, and a new car payment which he had to have all the time. Each was probably around $160 a month. I had to give him $80 per week and he was always broke by Wednesday. Then he would say, "if you don't give me more money I won't go to work. I'm not gonna be like those sick bastards that can't buy a cup of coffee."

More bragging on my brother. I don't think he had ever hung wallpaper that I knew of but when he came in my house and I was hanging wallpaper in my daughter's room he stood there and looked at it. Then he said which way do you hang, left or right? I said right and he said OK I'll hang left. The bedroom was done in no time and we met in the corner behind the door. The ideal place because if the match is off there it doesn't show.

When I was in the hospital running temperature for five days I kept thinking about Bill. I guess he's been in my subconscious mind all these years. When I first met him it was love at first sight for both of us. If I hadn't have been so desperate to get away from mom my life would have been so different. Now I wonder if everyone has someone they think about like I do Bill.

But what about me?

Still a little girl, that had to be a wife.
A little girl's decision, supposed to last through life.

Soon after we were married, his true ways begin to show,
as day by day, he turned into someone I didn't know.

He tells me that he owns me now. To him love means control.
The only way to get along, is do as I'm told.

But somewhere deep inside me, is this tiny little voice,
that is screaming silently, don't I have a choice?

Born with a broken heart and then blamed for crying

What happened to my younger years, and what about the love?
What happened to the hopes and plans that I kept dreaming of?

I woke today, and found I'm old, but what of yesterday?
You never think, while you're still young, of what I found today.

You always think, I still have time. I'll make my dreams come true.
You think some day is far away. Now it's caught up with you.

Too bad, it takes too many years, to realize this truth.
But, I hope that all my good years, weren't wasted on my youth.

Like most, I had a habit, of dwelling on the past.
Then thinking, oh well! Some day, but Someday came too fast.

Now I'm a different person, since I woke up today.
I can't wait one more minute, just waiting for some day.

I hope there are still tomorrows, some time to make things right.
Maybe a new beginning, is still within my sight.

I will not wait for some day. I'll push aside my fears,
and cherish every new day, because Someday now is here.

Chorus:
All my hopes and dreams are gone, of a life blessed from above,
because dreams turn into nightmares, in a home where there's no love.

Now threats and lies and cursing, are all he seems to know.
I know that all is lost now. I can't stay. Where do I go?

What happened to that little girl? Is she just lost in time?
Or is there enough left of her, somewhere within my mind?

Chorus:
But what about me? What about me?

Rhoda Lane

In the Corner of Your Heart

You run into an old friend, you haven't seen in years. He says, I've moved to small town USA. And you say hey!

I used to live there, but it's been a long, long time. And I've lost track of my friends, but by the way, maybe you have met them. Maybe they still care. Maybe they would like to see me too.
If I could take a day off, from my way to busy life, I could come see them, and visit you.

Old friend, I sure have missed you. Old friend, I really miss you too.

Old friend, I'm sorry that we've been so far apart. But, I've always kept you tucked away, in the corner of my heart.
Then you say Hey! I've got to go now. You turn to walk away, but realize you haven't asked about, the best friend in your whole life, and you hope he knows him too.

The friend that you can trust, without a doubt. And you say hey! Do you know Jesus? He says, it's been a long long time. I used to know him till I walked away.

But, I'm very glad you asked me, and I'll try hard to recall. I wonder if I still know how to pray?

Old friend, I sure have missed you. Old friend, I really miss you too. Old friend, I'm sorry that we've been so far apart. But, I've always kept you tucked away, in the corner of my heart.

Do you have Jesus tucked away, in the corner of your heart?

Wishes

I wish I had black hair, blonde, brown, or red hair, thick, thin, long, curly, or more.
I wish I had blue eyes, brown, Green, or Grey eyes, or just eyes that could see like before.

Wish I had a new car, a big house, a good wife. Wish I was a lottery winner.
I wish I was taller, young, older, or smaller, grown-up, wiser, richer, or thinner.

How many hours, have we wasted wishing, for things that are not meant to be?
And I think God would love to hear somebody say, thank you God, that you let me be me.

So I'm going to try, to trade wishes for prayers, 'cause prayer leads to God's perfect way.
And nothing in this life, matters at all, when we think what God's promised for someday.

Thank You Lord

For sleepless nights, that let me write, what I can't find by day
When I reach out in the darkness, you give me the words to say.

Then I'm awakened by the sound, as my pencil hits the floor.
And I realize, the sleepless nights, just make me love you more.

The old time picture frame

I'm thinking of the picture I was shown not long ago,
of someone I haven't known long, yet no all I need to know.

You see we share a grandson. I've come to know her in this way.
And each time she saw me with him, she never failed to say:

Thanks so much for taking such good care of our darling baby boy. And the look of love in her eyes, reflected my own joy.

She's ill now and her words are very hard to understand, except for love and oh so beautiful when she sees our little man.

 She looks beyond her pain, and for a little while, finds comfort in his baby talk, and pretty little smile.

A Special love is shared by those who truly love a child. It's a love that soothes the sick, calms the lonely, tames the wild.

Now as I think of that picture, the loving eyes there were the same, in the beautiful young face, in the old-time picture frame.

Believe and Receive

The plan of salvation is simple, but true.
Jesus died on the cross, for me and for you.

The first birth for all, is life maternal.
The rebirth from God, is life eternal.

So believe and receive. That's all you have to do.
Because when you accept Jesus, God accepts you.

I hope you liked my book.

Love,
Rhoda

CHAPTER 138

I FEEL AS THOUGH I SHOULD not complete this book without telling my visions. The first one was just in my mind. I kept seeing a combination baptismal and alter, in the corner of a ministry that we were involved in. I wanted a round galvanized tank. I was told they no longer made the round ones, only oval. After some persuading I got a salesman to call around for a round one. He found one in Kentucky and had it shipped. The next thing was wheels. They were very hard to find, and when I saw them I realized why. They were bright red, representative of the blood of Jesus. The handles for the lid had to be thorn or hedge. I called several places but couldn't find anything. Then one day the Holy Spirit prompted me to go to a small saw-mill in the country. The man explained that there was wood called thorny locust that had thorns sometimes a foot long. I thought maybe that was what the crown of thorns was made of for Jesus. The carpet color was **camel** which was fitting. We needed some rubber trim for the carpet, but the color that matched was only sold by the case. I asked the salesman if he would call the distributor and ask if he would sell me the five stripes we needed. When the distributor agreed, the store owner was amazed. I told him when God has a hand in something, He will work it out. The framework around it was iron with linen which was also hard to find at a reasonable price. When my husband and the man who ran the ministry finished everything we had a dedication ceremony before it was used. That's most of the details except of the dimensions also had to be certain numbers according to God's numbers, reminding me of the Tabernacle. I feel so honored that God would use me. Several people have been baptized in it, and the alter ledge is used quite often.

Later I started having real visions, not just in my head. One night I was watching the news then turned off the TV. Above the bed I started seeing something that looked like little clouds white with pastel colors in them. They kept getting thicker and were moving from North to South. They were so thick and unbelievably beautiful. When my husband walked in, I told him to lie down and look up. But he couldn't see them. Earlier I had put my hand in the clouds, and asked God if he had come to take me home. No answer so I said please don't take me yet. There are too many people who need me. The clouds faded out of sight.

The next vision was different shapes. More like clusters of grapes, and not much color.

The third vision, clouds again but less, and didn't last as long. The visions were all at night, and always in the bedroom.

The fourth vision was clouds again, but only on my side of the bed.

The fifth was completely different. It looked like a huge ball. It wasn't very colorful light gray or brown, but right in the middle across and a little lower, it was bright red, and sort of uneven. It looked like blood. The next day, I asked God what it meant. In my Spirit I heard. "Many are covered by the blood of Jesus. Many more are covered by the blood of evil.

My friend thinks the clouds was God allowing me to see the Shakina Glory.

Whatever they were, I thank my Lord for them.

Love Rhoda

www.ingramcontent.com/pod-product-compliance
Lightning Source LLC
Chambersburg PA
CBHW060357080526
44583CB00012B/361